In the Hollow of His Hand

Complete with Study Guide for
Individuals or Small Groups

In the Hollow of His Hand

ISBN 1-882185-55-2

Library of Congress Catalog Card Number: 97-69164

Cover illustration: Elizabeth Kramer
Cover painting: Irene Taylor
Editing: Katie Fitzgerald, Leda Shultz
Published by Cornerstone Publishing Inc., P.O. Box 7972, Louisville, Kentucky 40257.

Second Printing, 1998

Printed in the United States of America.

In the Hollow of His Hand

by
Irene Taylor

with
Kathie Fitzgerald

Foreword by Dolores Hayford

CONTENTS

DEDICATION

The book is dedicated to my husband Chris and my four daughters in grateful thanks for how much God has redeemed me through them.

They are the greatest gifts God has given me. They remind me of His acceptance and forgiveness — and they are living examples of how to be a whole person.

I also dedicate this book to my brother Michael as he lays dying of AIDS. How different his life would have been without the devastating influence of child and sexual abuse. May we meet again soon at the foot of the cross.

To God be the glory!

FOREWORD

For several years it has been my privilege to become friends with a great number of women who have experienced equally as troubled a life as the woman about whom, and by whom this story has been written. Though their experiences have been varied, my relationship with them has proven two things to me.

First, they are survivors. Given a different life setting, they would be the ones who, when washed overboard at sea, hang on to a bit of floating debris, catch fish with their bare hands, endure thirst, experience the sun's most devastating abuse, and live to tell us their incredibly wonderful story. These are the kind of people who, as prisoners of war, come home scarred and with health shot, but spirit strong. People like these endured the holocaust.

Second, I have found that "survivors" of abuse have something to give — if those of us who have been so "turned off" by the repugnance of what has happened to them would only take the time to know the person that is hidden inside! I have yet to discover one who is not bright and sensitive, capable of being a real contributor if given the chance and the necessary encouragement.

The author's purpose will have been lost if you do not find the bright thread of faith and trust which sustained her through years of horrible disappointment and pain.

The instigators of her suffering (now, nearly all of them!) not only know that they have her forgiveness, but they have found God's also. It is very difficult for most people to accept this as being "worth it all," but you can be sure it is her testimony.

The world immediately puts God on trial when reading a story like this. They do not consider the several adults in the story who could have and should have protected the children. Perhaps we, too, have been guilty of failing to speak up or become involved at some time or another in our lives.

God *did* deal with them through their own seared conscience, even when the raw deceitfulness of their hearts goaded them on their destructive way. Deep inside they knew that they were W-R-O-N-G!

A sad truth about fallen human nature is this: Even if God should miraculously intervene for the abused one, it seems to infuriate the offender only more deeply! There are other truths we also need to consider:

1. Neighbors do not intervene (usually for self-protective reasons.)

2. Society in general finds it so easy to "look the other way" because of our distaste for these scruffy looking kids — so difficult to love because of the belligerent attitude they have developed as a protective shield against our very evident distaste.

3. The far too frequent history of abuse continues if children such as these are taken from their families, only to fall into the hands of others who, at best, offer a sort of "antiseptic" acceptance, or, at worst, are abusers themselves! Usually, neither attitude is intentional, but most people are simply emotionally incapable of understanding and giving what these kids need so badly.

4. A really "hard nut to swallow" is this: God's heart aches for the abuser, just as it does for the abused! We are all guilty of abusing His plan for man. That is why He sacrificed His Son to redeem us all. The cold, hard fact is this: The way to end the behavior of abusers is to bring them into the household of faith. Most of them know all too well that they need God, but it is very hard for them to accept the fact that He would love and accept them!

5. It is usually "blind-faith-against-all-odds" that prevails in the final analysis. Like Irene, most abused people have their times of anger over the unfairness of life. By choice, at times, they join the crowd, hoping to forget the pain. But, as with her, these are times of human weakness, and the real survivors quickly recognize the futility of such a choice. When no one else is able to see God in the midst, survivors do, and press on.

Where is God while all this is going on? He moves among us, waiting for us to be His voice, His hands, His feet! Most places of greatest service to God are not up-front, spot-lighted ministry. In fact, Jesus has very pointedly said, "In as much as you have done it to the least of these, you have done it unto me." How you and I receive the abuser is as important to God as how we comfort and encourage the abused.

As you read this story, let there run an under-current of thought about your community, your church, and your family. We can make a difference in these pitiable situations if we will be more like Jesus to the people who so desperately need His love and healing.

— Dolores Hayford, teacher, evangelist,
and mother of Jack Hayford

PREFACE

This book is a work of non-fiction and has been written with the maximum possible amount of accuracy. My prayerful intent has been to tell the story exactly as it happened, without exaggeration or embellishment. It is the story of my life as I remember it, through the eyes of my childhood. Every detail of this story has been included with the prayerful guidance of the Lord Jesus.

I am grateful that my children did not ever have to suffer like my sisters, brothers, and I did. And I know that God has used me to break the cycle of generations of dysfunctional behavior: abuse, alcoholism, poverty, perversion and neglect within my family. My girls are whole and healthy because of what God has done. How unwhole they could have been if I didn't have Jesus, if I didn't know His grace, and if I didn't have Him whispering in my ear each day, "You can be a good mom. Even though you don't know how, you can do it. I'll show you how, Irene." Even now, when my kids are teenagers, He continues to say, "You can do it. You can do it."

I've had that encouragement every day of my life, and it's helped me to keep things in perspective and to not go off the deep end because of the things that have happened in my past.

I also thank the Lord for sending another comforter, Kathie Fitzgerald, my friend. We have spent many happy hours working on this project. I think of her as my sister.

Thanks also to Dolores Hayford for writing the foreword to introduce this book. Her prayerful reading and her words of encouragement came at a most opportune moment.

In the writing of this book, Kathie and I were accorded the most gracious and prayerful help from Marilyn Schneider, a dear friend in Christ and one who encouraged us to go on toward the mark. How we love and appreciate her.

Kathie and I wish to express additional thanks to the following persons for their invaluable help in editing the manuscript: Rev. Everest "Zip" and Milly Zediker, Rev. Don and Jo Brunk, Glenn and Alice Shultz, Rev. Chris Taylor, and Tim Fitzgerald. Their prayerful input helped us clarify and make certain that my story was told with accuracy and in accordance with Biblical principles. Thanks also to Stella Scruggs for her technical support and the use of transcription equipment which saved us many hours of valuable time.

The following song — "'Til the Storm Passes By" — accurately expresses my life. I can remember my grandmother singing this song to me when I was a child. I begin the book with this song, hoping that it will express to some extent the way that God moved me through the horrible circumstance of my childhood. I hope that it will also encourage you as you journey through your life.

Irene June Taylor

'Til the Storm Passes By

In the dark of the midnight have I oft hid my face,
While the storms howl above me and there's no hiding place.
Mid the crash of the thunder Precious Lord hear my cry,
Keep me safe 'til the storm passes by.

Many times Satan whispers there is no use to try,
For there's no end of sorrow, there's no hope by and by.
But I know Thou art with me and tomorrow I'll rise,
Where the storms never darken the sky.

When the long night is ended and the storms come no more
Let me stand in Thy presence on that bright peaceful shore.
In that land where the tempest never comes, Lord may I
Dwell with Thee when the storm passes by.

'Til the storm passes over, 'til the thunder sounds no more
'Til the clouds roll forever from the sky.
Hold me fast, let me stand **in the hollow of Thy hand**,
Keep me safe 'til the storm passes by.

ASTORIA

Hear, O Lord, when I cry aloud; have mercy and be gracious to me and answer me! You have said, Seek you My face — inquire for and require My presence [as your vital need]. My heart says to You, Your face [Your presence], Lord, will I seek, inquire for and require [of necessity and on the authority of Your Word]. Hide not Your face from me; turn not Your servant away in anger, You Who have been my help! Cast me not off, neither forsake me, O God of my salvation!

Psalm 27:7-10 AMP

Water sloshed against the pilings as Irene and Pud carefully picked their way along the dilapidated old dock. Here and there whole pieces of board had fallen through, splashing down to litter the floor of the Columbia River. In the distance the fresh river water mingled with ocean saltiness. Tall ships and barges anchored midstream waited for tugboats to pull them out to sea or drag them into the deep river channel on their way to Portland.

At the end of the dock, Irene settled into her favorite position, dangling her feet off the wooden structure. The damp planks felt chilly in the late evening, and the clean, fresh wind caressed her young face.

"I'm sure glad you're here with me, Pud," Irene said. "Friends are hard to come by. If you find a good one, you should work real hard to keep him."

Pud looked at Irene in mute agreement. Irene thought carefully for a few minutes about this idea, then changed the topic as if some painful impression made the subject uncomfortable.

"Those sea gulls are lucky. They can fly around and not have a care in the world," Irene said.

They watched as a giant bird dive-bombed the river surface picking up refuse or an occasional fish for his dinner. Other birds circled trying to snatch a prize from his beak.

"When I grow up everything will be different. I'll have money. I'll have shoes — lots of shoes. And dresses, all colors. And I'm going to sing for the President and on television." She rambled on and on, her voice mingling with the sound of wind, water, and waves. Here was peace. Here was a refuge.

The sky darkened over the glistening water. Slowly fog and chill rose from the surface and rolled ponderously inland, darkening the flashes of sunset and making the sky a red, fiery furnace. Now Irene could barely distinguish the neighboring dock, only yards away, or the huge old cannery, now crumbling and falling in disrepair. Fear crept into her voice.

"Come on, Pud. We'd better get going." She carefully picked hand holds on the slick, mossy surface of the dock and got herself upright, then skillfully made her way between the missing boards and back to dry land.

By then it was dark. "Come on, Puddles. Let's go. You know I'm afraid of the dark." Puddles' blond- and white-haired body bounced along close behind Irene, his short dog legs pumping hard trying to keep up.

She headed up the alley, her feet pounding on the planks that formed a bridge of sorts over the constant run off flowing down to the street. Apartment houses crowded against the narrow alleyway providing cheap housing for people unfortunate enough to have to live there.

She clambered over a fence and up more planks to the three-story abandoned bordello her family called home. The original white paint still showed, but wind and rain had aged the house to the color of dead, gray ocean wood. A front porch led into a large open living room. The kitchen was small — in fact, the house had probably never needed a kitchen before they moved in. Upstairs were seven tiny bedrooms with not a single closet.

Irene quietly eased the door shut behind her, scouting the territory to avoid potential trouble. She never knew what she would find when she came home. She turned toward the stairs hoping to escape to her room before she was discovered. But it was too late. Her mother Evelyn stalked in from the kitchen.

"Where have you been? You've been gone for hours. I waited and waited. Now get in here." She held the broomstick in her hand and headed for Irene.

"I'm sorry, Mom. I'm here now. What do you want me for this time? What did I do?" Irene searched her mind to remember what rule she might have broken.

"You're going to clean this house. You're going to stay right here and take care of things. The kids aren't even fed. Where have you been? I'm going to the Desmona, and I'm late now." Irene sighed and headed for the kitchen.

"Why do you always have to go there, Mom?" she said under her breath.

"What did you say?" Evelyn headed for Irene, the broomstick flailing. "How dare you!" Irene dashed for the kitchen, but not before one powerful whack struck her squarely across the back.

"I didn't mean anything, Mom. Just go ahead, and I'll fix dinner." She held up her hands as Evelyn pounded her on the side of the head. Blow after blow descended from her mother's powerful arm as Irene dodged and cowered to protect herself. She covered her ears to diminish the damage, but the broom hit her straight across the nose. Blood squirted down her face and shirt, and tears wet her cheeks.

"If you don't stop that crying, I'm going to hit you again."

"Okay, Mom." Irene forced herself to control the wracking emotion, knowing that something worse could follow. She grabbed a rag to wipe the blood from her face and neck. "I'm okay now, Mom. You go on down to the bar. I'll go feed the kids."

Evelyn stood for a moment, deciding whether more punishment was warranted. Irene looked at her and forced a small smile in anticipation of her mother's departure.

"I'm doing it, Mom. You can go now." She watched as her mother sighed, the last of her anger dissolving in expectation of her night at the bar.

Irene leaned against the kitchen cabinet and watched through

17

the window as her mother sauntered down the alley to the Desmona Tavern. Tears splattered down, mingling with the blood on her face — and she cried out to the God she had met as a small child.

"Dear Jesus, can't you stop this? Please help us." She wondered, not for the first time, how their lives had gotten to this place, this sad and unhappy existence. How did this all begin?

RIDGE

He hath made every thing beautiful in His time: also He hath set the world in their heart, so that no man can find out the work that God maketh from the beginning to the end.

Ecclesiastes 3:11 KJV

"For I know the plans I have for you," declares the Lord, "plans to prosper you and not to harm you, plans to give you hope and a future. Then you will call upon me and come and pray to me, and I will listen to you. You will seek me and find me when you seek me with all your heart. I will be found by you," declares the Lord, "and will bring you back from captivity."

Jeremiah 28:11-14 NIV

Irene's mother, Evelyn, was born in the small town of Ridge, Montana. Her grandparents were homesteaders in the area, and life was rough, filled with hard work and very little fun or relief from the backbreaking labor necessary to feed a family. It was an existence that drove people either to inner strength of character, or to the bottle.

The men in Evelyn's family chose that fiery amber liquid that promised them brief deliverance from their hardships. Even as a child, she remembered her father coming home falling down drunk. He would load his pistol and shoot imaginary rats off the wall while Evelyn cowered in fear under the table.

Eventually Evelyn's mother, Ada, escaped from those circumstances, took her children, and moved to McMinnville, Oregon. There Ada met and married Ernie.

At first their lives were much improved. Ernie did not drink and desired to be a good father to the children. But he had served in World War I, where he sustained serious physical and emotional injuries.

Evelyn and her stepfather developed a stormy relationship. She was a rebellious teenager, balking at even the most reasonable regulation of her behavior. She was loud and crude and rude. She dated the wildest boys, including one teenager who was jailed for murdering his high school principal.

She did, at one point, attend an Assembly of God church during her high school years, but only because of a dare by some students. The day she went, she sat in the back laughing and giggling with her friends. Near the end of the sermon her attention was caught by the words of the pastor. As the altar call was given, she found herself at the altar with tears running down her face, asking for forgiveness.

This brief experience, however, did not result in a change in her behavior. Evelyn constantly came home drunk. She refused to attend high school. Ernie was flabbergasted at her conduct. They argued and fought. Sometimes, he would physically beat her into submission, which drove Evelyn farther away.

Eventually, at age 17, she met Dwayne, a feisty drinking Irish boy, who had barely made it through third grade. She did not love Dwayne, but saw their relationship as a way out of her family life, away from her parents. Dwayne felt sorry for her and wanted to rescue her from the stormy family. They eloped.

PALMER

If I take the wings of the morning and dwell in the utter-most parts of the sea, even there shall Your hand lead me, and Your right hand shall hold me. If I say, Surely the darkness shall cover me, and the night shall be the only light about me, even the darkness hides nothing from You, but the night shines as the day; the darkness and the light are both alike to You. For You did form my inward parts, You did knit me together in my mother's womb. I will confess and praise You, for You are fearfully wonderful, and for the awful wonder of my birth! Wonderful are Your works, and that my inner self knows right well. My frame was not hidden from You, when I was being formed in secret and intricately and curiously wrought (as if embroidered with various colors) in the depths of the earth [a region of darkness and mystery]. Your eyes saw my unformed substance, and in Your book all the days of my life were written, before ever they took shape, when as yet there was none of them.

Psalms 139:9-16 AMP

Evelyn and Dwayne first moved in with his parents and near his brother's family. Dwayne looked up to his older brother Harry and listened with excitement as he talked incessantly about the Alaskan Gold Rush. He made it sound as if piles of nuggets lay around on the ground just waiting for someone to pick them up. Shortly after Evelyn and Dwayne's marriage, Harry, his wife, Lottie, and their daughter, Sharon, headed off in search of their dreams, north to Alaska.

Even though the illusion of riches far exceeded the harsh realities of Alaska, Harry sent word to Dwayne that there was a lot of money to be made. He was working in the coal mines but often gold, diamonds, and other gems were taken out of the mines. He neglected to mention that these riches were owned by the coal company.

Dwayne and Evelyn waited until after the birth of their daughter Shirley to follow Harry and Lottie to Alaska. Dwayne worked in the mines, and they lived in a company house near the hundreds of other displaced workers. The labor was long and cold and difficult.

They lived in a tiny one-bedroom house with no indor plumbing. A coal-oil stove heated the 20-foot by 20-foot home, located near Harry and Lottie. But as the truth about living in Alaska became more apparent, the two families no longer got along.

Dwayne would get coal from work to heat the house, but as time went by and the hardship took its toll, he preferred to spend his time instead at the company bar.

Evelyn became pregnant for a second time and gave birth to a premature son who lived only two days. Dwayne expressed mixed feelings. One part of him desperately wanted a son, and another part wanted to escape the growing burden of family responsibility.

When Evelyn got pregnant the third time, pain and fear pushed Dwayne to the extreme. He no longer wanted the child they had, much less another one. Evelyn thought that Dwayne secretly put poisoned mushrooms into their evening meal, making her deathly ill and causing her to lose another son.

Evelyn felt the pressure of Dwayne's despair. She lived in fear of becoming pregnant again. Two years after the birth of Shirley, and following the loss of the two boy babies, she became pregnant again, with Irene. She held the knowledge back from Dwayne as long as possible, but eventually told him. For a time Dwayne controlled his reaction to her pregnancy, but when Evelyn was seven and a half months pregnant, she and Dwayne had a violent argument.

Dwayne grabbed Evelyn as she stood on the porch at Harry and Lottie's house. He shouted at her and then slapped her, knocking her off the porch and onto the ground four steps down. He stalked off towards the coal mine to go to work.

She returned home to rest, but within hours Evelyn felt the growing pressure of labor pains. She was still six weeks from her due date, and fear rose in her heart. She struggled across the housing compound back to Lottie's house, and her sister-in-law drove her to the company hospital.

The doctors had little hope that the baby would survive. Later that afternoon, April 30, 1953, she gave birth to a four-pound, 10-ounce screaming baby. Dwayne finally came to the hospital the next morning. They named the child "Ione" after a distant relative, but a nurse misspelled the name on the birth certificate, so they went home with baby "Irene."

At times, after the baby came, life was good. Evelyn loved music and would turn up the radio in its old wooden cabinet, singing and dancing around the tiny house. She knew all the words to dozens of Gershwin songs and sang them out loud, to the delight of the two babies.

Dwayne loved music too. On good evenings he would come home and sit in the rocking chair with both children in his lap. He would pull out his precious harmonica and perform tunes from his childhood. The beautiful notes would hang in the air, buffering them from the harsh difficulties of survival in Alaska.

But with the new baby, pressures eventually increased in their household. Shirley was old enough to eat whatever food was scantily available, but Irene was allergic to both breast and cow's milk. She needed goat's milk in order to survive, but that cost money. Milk was available from a goat farm, but it required a weekly trip. As time passed, both Dwayne and Evelyn spent more and more of the household money in the local tavern. Sometimes Evelyn would hide milk money for the weekly trip, only to discover that Dwayne had taken the money to the bar. Sometimes neither of them worried about the milk money.

Without intervention the baby would die, but a guardian angel came to their aid. Irene and Shirley's 11-year-old cousin, Sharon, noticed the two children were left alone for hours each evening while Dwayne and Evelyn sat at the bar. She came to the house each afternoon after school.

She saw their filthy clothes and unchanged diapers, so she bathed and cleaned them. She observed how hungry they were. She saved her lunch money to buy goat's milk for Irene. When there was coal, she stoked a tiny fire.

Irene's baby bed was a drawer in the dresser. A soft blanket was used to line the drawer. It became a symbol of a complete and utter terror that would haunt Irene into her adult years.

As the pressure grew on Evelyn — lack of money, months of freezing cold, the absence of friends or family to comfort her — tension mounted. She became moody, going into a rage over her problems. Dwayne started disappearing for days at a time, turning up in Anchorage without remembering how he got there.

When Irene's stomach cramped from her allergy to milk, she would cry for hours. Eventually Evelyn would stamp across the room and slam the drawer shut with the baby still inside. As baby Irene stared up in the dark, terror muted her cries. She could hardly breathe from fear. Her baby stomach ached with the cramps from drinking the cow's milk, but she made no sound.

Hours later Sharon would come from school to find two-year-old Shirley sobbing on the bed and Irene still shut up in the dresser drawer. Gently she would remove the baby, comfort Shirley, then clean and feed them. She was powerless to do more.

When Irene was 10 months old, her grandmother Ada visited Alaska. She loved little Irene and showered her with affection. Evelyn was offended by this attachment to Irene, and she became more devoted to Shirley, her first born.

Good Samaritan

Tiny, cold, wet, and crying
Weeping voice longing to be heard
Dresser for a bed
No cradle for this head.
Life anew, in pink not blue.

Will this noise ever cease?
Shut her in! Shut her in!
Murky shadows

Dark comes in
Noise grows dim
Life anew, in pink not blue.

Angels whisper
Go and find! Go and find!
Life's not kind
Light comes in
A Sharon grin
Life anew, in pink not blue.

Irene Taylor

Shirley was an adorable little child, blond and blue eyed like her namesake Shirley Temple. She seemed able to withstand physical deficiencies better than her sister. She had an easier time than Irene, having no milk allergy. And without the sporadic stomach cramps she had a better disposition. These factors reinforced her mother's approval of Shirley and growing irritation with Irene.

Ada recognized in Irene the growing signs of disease, her legs twisting with rickets from vitamin deficiency, her hair lusterless from malnutrition. She spoke gently to Evelyn, trying not to offend her strong-willed daughter. How could she help? Did Evelyn want to come home with her? How could she keep the children in this condition?

Evelyn grew fearful of her questions, wondering if her mother wanted to take the children away from her. As her growing alcoholism augmented her fears, she rejected her mother's offer of help and sent her away.

In the two years that followed, the situation worsened. Weeks would go by with less coal for the fire. Dwayne raged against his "entrapment" of family and responsibility. Now, not only did he torment Evelyn about any future pregnancy, but he threatened the lives of the children and Evelyn, promising to kill them all.

Evelyn knew that the menace was real. He gained courage from the whiskey, and she was sure that, at some point, he would lose control and murder them. As her stomach swelled with yet another new life, she prayed to the God she had met briefly in that church in high school, a God in which she did not completely believe. She begged Him for a way out.

VERNONIA

For the Son of man is come to save that which was lost. How think ye? If a man have a hundred sheep, and one of them be gone astray, doth he not leave the ninety and nine, and goeth into the mountains, and seeketh that which is gone astray? And if so be that he find it, verily I say unto you, he rejoiceth more of that sheep, than of the ninety and nine which went not astray. Even so it is not the will of your Father which is in heaven, that one of these little ones should perish.

Matthew 18:11-14 KJV

So Evelyn swallowed her pride and went home. Her parents met her at the small Portland airport and took her and the children home to their attractive white house in Vernonia, Oregon.

There was a white picket fence and rows of carefully tended roses and other flowers. A huge old tree shadowed the front yard. Inside, the polished wood floors were covered with heavy deep rugs. The house smelled of generous home cooked meals and freshly cut flowers.

The children thought they were in wonderland. Their grandparents showered them with new clothes and their first pairs of shoes. At night, they took baths in hot water, put on fresh, clean pajamas and snuggled deep into sheets that smelled of sunshine and fresh air. There were thick blankets on the beds.

In the morning, the children would come down into the living room and sit close to the oil stove, drinking in the blessed warmth. Ernie made a tiny rocking chair for each child to sit in by the old stove.

For the first time the children had toys, dolls, and a little glass tea set. Ernie made a small table and chairs for the girls, and they spent hours pouring imaginary liquids into the delicate China. Ada made outfits for their dolls, complete with diapers.

A few months later, Evelyn gave birth to a son, Michael, and the house was filled with the laughter and voices of happy children. Dwayne came to visit briefly, to see his new son and check on the family. But when Ernie demanded that Dwayne help support the children, there was a terrible fight. Dwayne did not want the responsibility of children or a wife, so he left them alone again and was no longer a part of their family. Soon after, Evelyn and Dwayne divorced.

Ernie and Evelyn disagreed vehemently on the issue of discipline. He thought she spanked the children too hard and needed to control her temper with them. He believed that she vented strong emotion and over-reacted to their small indiscretions.

At Ernie's insistence Irene was taken to doctors and treated for rickets. They put her in heavy leg braces in an attempt to align her twisted limbs. She slept in shoes with a cross bar to straighten her crooked feet. She thrived with the attention, both physical and emotional.

Irene and Ernie developed a special relationship. He took her to stores with him, running errands. In the evenings he sang with her and discovered that she had a quick memory for music. He serenaded her with songs about Jesus — "I Come to the Garden Alone," "Jesus Loves Me," and "What a Friend We Have in Jesus" — and children's songs, such as:

> *The robin hopped along on the lawn,*
> *The robin hopped along on the lawn,*
> *And he sang a jubilee in the crooked apple tree.*
> *For the winter, don't you see, it was gone.*

It delighted him that Irene could hear a song only twice and remember every word and note. They became inseparable. This made Evelyn nervous.

Ernie's best friend Jake lived right across the street and Ernie and Irene often visited him. The men planned projects and built things together with Irene tagging along to watch.

In Jake's yard grew a giant plum tree. In spring, it hung heavy with fruit. While Ernie and Jake plotted their projects, Irene savored the succulent fruit. Ernie noticed her enjoyment and started calling her "Little Prune."

Some mornings she would sneak out of bed very early, dragging her long heavy flannel gown along the pavement to the street. She would knock on the door saying, "Mr. Jake, can I have a plum please?" Jake would laugh, pick her some fresh fruit, and load it into the apron Irene formed with her nightgown.

The years had softened Ernie. He and Ada had come to know the Lord Jesus, and he was far more tolerant of people. He regretted the beatings he had given Evelyn when she was younger. But even though he grieved over his past actions, he still could not understand why Evelyn preferred the tavern over caring for her children. He noticed not only the excessive spankings, but the basic neglect of the children's needs.

Ernie would hold his tongue until he thought he would explode, then make another attempt to talk to Evelyn about the children. Irene would come downstairs after one of their repeated "talks" and find him, head bent over his hands at the kitchen table, crying tears over his still wayward step-daughter.

About 18 months after they moved in, Ernie took Irene downtown shopping to just look around. He noticed a sale table piled high with discount children's clothing. Irene's pants had large holes in the knees, so he bought her a new pair. He paid less than a dollar.

When they arrived home, Evelyn asked why he hadn't bought a pair of pants for Shirley. Ernie had simply not thought of it. He didn't mean to slight Shirley. He just noticed the hole in Irene's pants.

Evelyn grew angry, accusing him of playing favorites, of not loving her Shirley as much as he loved Irene. The argument escalated, getting totally out of control.

Angry words echoed, breaking the peaceful spirit in the household. At the end of the fight, Evelyn packed her bags, called a friend for a ride, and left with the children.

HOOD RIVER

[O Lord] remember [earnestly] my affliction and my misery, my wandering and outcast state, the wormwood and the gall. My soul has them continually in remembrance and is bowed down within me. But this I recall, therefore have I hope and expectation; It is of the Lord's mercies and loving-kindnesses that we are not consumed, because His (tender) compassions fail not. They are new every morning; great and abundant is Your stability and faithfulness. The Lord is my portion or share, says my living being; therefore will I hope in Him and expectantly wait for him. . . . It is good for a man that he bear the yoke [of divine disciplinary dealings] in his youth.

Lamentations 3:19-24,27 AMP

Even a child is known by his doings, whether his work be pure, and whether it be right.

Proverbs 20:11 KJV

In Hood River, Oregon, Evelyn searched desperately for affordable housing, settling at last for a shack behind the Assembly of God church. The house had a small living room and one tiny bedroom. They had little furniture. A single bed and a dresser crowded the bedroom. A couch, table, and old wood radio occupied the living room. The bedroom closet was large enough for a mattress. This became the children's bedroom. They owned two blankets, one for Evelyn and the other for Shirley, Irene and Michael on their bed in the closet.

Behind the dilapidated shack were oil drums on tall legs where the children played. The yard was not fenced, and the children were free to run wild in the neighborhood.

On Saturday evenings Evelyn would remind the children that they were to get up and go to church the next morning. Then she would head down to the local saloon to find adult company.

There was no baby-sitter, no friendly neighbor to look in on the children. As evening drew closer, the children — Shirley (age 5), Irene (age 3), and Michael (age 1) — huddled together, dreading the coming dark. They turned on the radio, listening to the only available station which played opera on Saturday nights. After the station ended broadcast they snuggled close in the center of Evelyn's bed, trying to stay warm. Irene clung to the doll given to her by Grandma Ada. Sounds echoed throughout the house, and the children imagined all sorts of impending danger — including the boogie man, the devil, and an escaped lunatic, all intent on murder.

Eventually Evelyn stumbled home, kicking the children out of her bed and into the closet. They huddled in the darkness, still consumed with fear as Evelyn snored in oblivion.

The next morning, Shirley and Irene dressed Mike and got ready for church. They put on their clothes which were rapidly becoming too small, as there were no new clothes after they left their grandparents' home. They washed their faces and combed each other's hair, carefully keeping quiet as their mother slept. Then they walked to the front of the tall new church building.

They attended Sunday school and heard stories about Jesus and how He loved them. The people were kind to the children, and patient with their questions. They taught them how to pray and ask the Lord Jesus for help in their daily lives. They told the children that Jesus cared about every detail and problem they had, and that Jesus also loved their mom.

When church time came, the children sat near the front. Irene loved the music and would lift her voice to sing as loud as she could, so that Jesus could hear. She learned all the choruses and many hymns. And while she sang, she could feel the presence of

Jesus, almost like He was sitting right beside her. She felt better in church than any other place in her life.

One Sunday, Irene stood beside Shirley as they sang "Come Into My Heart Lord Jesus." She stood on tiptoe to see over the pew and sang the words with all her heart. "Come in today, come in to stay." On that day, her heart swelled with a feeling of peace, and she knew that with Jesus in her heart, she would never be alone again.

Outwardly, nothing changed. Evelyn's growing dependence on alcohol brought more rage and temper into their lives. She spanked the children with all her might for the slightest disobedience, leaving bruises and marks on their bodies. On one occasion, the children were eating potato soup, which they ate morning, noon and night for weeks on end. Irene dipped a small piece of bread into the soup, but Evelyn did not see the bread and thought Irene was putting her fingers in the bowl.

She screamed at the top of her lungs, "You don't put your hands in the soup. Can't you get anything right, Irene?" She knocked Irene out of her chair and onto the floor. Then she beat her until her body swelled with purple bruises.

That Christmas, Evelyn's family had absolutely nothing but the leaking roof over their heads. A few days before Christmas even the potato soup gave out. They had applied for welfare, but had not yet been accepted. Evelyn sat at the table and stared into space. Pride prevented her from returning to her mother and stepfather. There was nowhere else to turn.

In desperation she called out to God, her voice carrying through the house, "If there really is a God up there, I need Your help right now. If you ever really existed then please send us some food. Help me with the children. It's Christmas time. I'd like to get them something. I'm not asking for much." She prayed and got out an old Bible that her mother had given her. She read parts of scripture out loud, searching for some magic button to push, something to move the hand of God.

That very afternoon a soft knock sounded at the door. Evelyn looked out the window suspiciously, then cautiously opened the door. A tall thin young man with the kindest eyes stood there smiling at her.

"I heard you needed food, and I wanted to help."

"What?" Evelyn looked at him in shock.

"Here, take this while I bring some more from the car," He shoved the box into her arms and turned back to his vehicle. He brought in two more boxes, and on his final trip, he carried in a small Christmas tree, placed it on the table and left.

Evelyn looked in the boxes, eyeing the fresh turkey, potatoes, carrots, cereal, milk, bread, candy canes, toilet paper and canned goods. The children smelled the pungent odor of fresh oranges.

"God does hear! God does listen!" she said in amazement. Then she fell on her chair sobbing into her folded arms.

It was, without doubt, the most magnificent Christmas of their lives. Evelyn set up the tree and looked around the house for tidbits to decorate it. She and the children made ornaments out of newspaper and aluminum foil from the boxes of food. And when the tree was covered with their handmade creations, she sat at the table and opened the Bible to the Christmas story. As she read the story, she understood for the first time about the angel who came to Mary and then to Joseph.

"That man at the door was an angel of mercy," she said. "We need to do something very special to remember him."

Using pipe cleaners, she constructed an angel for the top of their tree, so they would never forget God's mercy in their deepest time of need.

Eventually Evelyn was accepted for welfare. This brought some financial relief and supplied periodic food. On the day the check came, Evelyn would take the children downtown while she cashed the check and bought supplies. This day evolved into a real celebration called "Ice Cream Day." She would take Shirley by one hand, carry Michael on her arm, and tell Irene to hang on to Shirley.

The trail to town wound down an abrupt hillside path through heavy brush and large thick trees. The growth was so dense that dark shadows obscured the steep wooden staircase. As they started down the slippery incline, the dense branches reached across the path and wiped their cold wet fingers on Irene's face. She could not see the steps in front of her.

Evelyn noticed her hesitation and turned to her with encouragement, "We're going on the stairs now, Irene. Don't be afraid. I have your hand. You won't fall. I can see the stairs and where

I'm going." Irene trusted her mother to lead them safely down the hundreds of stairs.

In years to come, this memory would stand as a symbol of how God would lead her through times of great difficulty. She took her mother's hand, as she would later take His, and trust that together they would get to the end of the pathway.

Near the end of the path, the trees spread out, and warm sun broke through to light their way. They headed down the street for the bank to cash the welfare check. Irene slipped her hand out of her mother's and walked along behind.

She noticed a man standing by a mailbox, leaning heavily against it. His clothes were filthy and he smelled of alcohol and perspiration. Evelyn hurried by, but Irene walked straight up to the man and started a conversation.

"Hey, Mr. Bum, are you my daddy?" He looked at her, with curious eyes. Evelyn ran back to grab Irene's hand.

"Come on, Irene. You know better than to talk to strangers."

"But, Mommy, you said my daddy was a drunken bum. Was that my daddy?" Evelyn shook her head with exasperation.

"No, you stupid girl. That's not your daddy. He doesn't live anywhere near here. Do you want any ice cream or not?"

"Sure I do! But where did I come from, Mommy?" Irene asked.

"Oh, it doesn't matter. You were born on the beach underneath a rock. Stop this nonsense, and let's go."

As a child, Irene hated winter. Her joints ached in the cold, and it seemed that she was more susceptible than normal to childhood illness. She had constant colds, asthma, and repeated cases of the normal childhood afflictions: mumps, scarlet fever, rubella, and numerous bouts of pneumonia. But the children were never taken to the doctor unless the illness appeared life threatening.

Before the widespread use of penicillin, the chief treatment for pneumonia was the use of an oxygen tent. Irene spent several weeks at a time in the oxygen tent at the nearby hospital in Hood River. These times of sickness were very hard on young Irene. Her mother had a strong aversion to hospitals and refused to spend time in them. When Irene became so ill she could barely breathe, Evelyn would take her to the emergency room, drop her off with the doctors, and go home.

At times, Irene would spend a week or 10 days alone in the

hospital under the oxygen tent, with absolutely no visitors. She was too young to fully understand what was happening and lived in constant fear that she had been sent there to die. The nurses were kind to her, but she wanted the comfort of her own mother.

Once her grandparents found out that she was in the hospital, they came to care for her. Grandma Ada sat for days on end by Irene's bed, comforting her and talking to her. She would stroke Irene's hair and pray for her. The child was overjoyed, and she got well quickly. But Evelyn resented this intrusion into her care of the family. Again she feared that her parents would try to take the children from her.

When Irene was four, Evelyn went to a dance in town and met William, a kind and gentle man with a huge jolly laugh. She enjoyed his company, and soon he was a fixture in their lives. In only a short period of time they decided to marry. The children were very excited.

On the day of the wedding, all three children woke up with chicken pox and were unable to attend. Under William's influence, someone was sent to watch over the children during the ceremony. It was one of the first times they had a baby-sitter — some things were really changing.

A few days after the wedding William came to the shack and packed the children and their few boxes of belongings into his car. Then they drove 20 miles to his parent's home in Parkdale, Oregon.

PARKDALE

*My steps have held to your paths; my feet have not slipped, I call upon you, O God, for you will answer me; give ear to me and hear my prayer. Show the wonder of your great love, you who save by your right hand those who take refuge in you from their foes. **Keep me as the apple of your eye; hide me in the shadow of your wings** from the wicked who assail me, from my mortal enemies who surround me. They close up their callous hearts, and their mouths speak with arrogance. They have tracked me down, they now surround me, with eyes alert, to throw me to the ground. They are like a lion hungry for prey, like a great lion crouching in cover. Rise up, O Lord, confront them, bring them down; rescue me from the wicked by your sword. O Lord, by your hand save me from such men, from men of this world whose reward is in this life.*

Psalm 17:5-14a NIV

Ye shall not afflict any widow, or fatherless child. If you afflict them in any wise, and they cry at all to me, I will surely hear their cry; and my wrath shall wax hot, and I will kill you with the sword; and your wives shall be widows, and your children fatherless.

Exodus 22:22-24 KJV

At first, Irene's family moved in with William's parents in the large old beautiful home on the government camp road to Mount Hood. It was a mansion to the children. After two years of destitution in Hood River, they reveled in clean sheets which their grandmother hung outside to smell of the fresh, sweet orchard winds. There were thick towels and comfortable beds. Grandma Winifred cooked plentiful fresh food and the children were charmed by her quiet, gentle kindness. Grandfather Jess had a large orchard and spent his free time cutting rocks in a small shed out back.

William prepared a home for the family across the field from his parent's residence. The plain building had a large living room with patterned swirling blue linoleum on the floor. There were no rugs, but the living room was relatively warm as the house was heated by a wood stove. The kitchen was smaller, but had a large table in the middle, with chairs for everyone to sit and eat. White porcelain fixtures and aqua painted cabinets created an attractive atmosphere. For the first time they had an electric stove in the kitchen.

At first, life in their new household was full of joy and hope. Evelyn seemed very happy with her new husband. She waxed the linoleum floors to a brilliant shine. And the children would put on socks to run and slide across the slick floors.

In the yard there were all kinds of flowers. Evelyn loved the irises and lilac bushes that grew in profusion around the front of the house. A big old weeping willow tree stood in the corner of the lawn where the kids played on stick horses under its shady branches. There were many good times here.

Irene grew close to her Grandma Winifred. She was a quiet person with a submissive nature. They sewed together and did projects around the house. One afternoon they glued stars to the ceiling of the downstairs bedroom, and when the lights were turned off, they glowed in the darkness. She read stories to Irene, and at one point she read all of *Huckleberry Finn* aloud to her. She was a very gracious lady.

Some afternoons Irene would nap at their house, lying down on the couch and pretending she was asleep, just so she wouldn't have to go home. Her grandmother would get a blanket to put over her, and finally she would drift to sleep. Irene reveled in even that small affection. She adored Grandma Winifred.

Winifred had little patience with Evelyn. Irene was a clumsy child, falling and injuring herself with some regularity. Her balance was not good, a physical reminder of the childhood rickets and malnutrition that had twisted her legs. She developed a form of juvenile arthritis, which caused constant inflammation in her joints. When Irene fell and hurt herself Evelyn would get angry and slap her across the head with a book. This made Winifred furious.

Irene was a lonely child. Her only real friends were animals. Her cat, Snowball, a wild white creature with one black spot on his back, would have nothing to do with the other children. He was always available to Irene, comforting her in the absence of other friends. Often she sat under the front porch, hidden from view by the lattice that lined it on three sides. She daydreamed with her purring friend, and talked out loud about ballroom dancing, her mind's eye picturing herself gracefully gliding across a highly polished wood floor in the arms of a handsome stranger. Snowball offered no judgments, only support for the lonely child.

Hidden under the porch with her cat, Irene would talk to God about her life and the difficulties she faced every day. Memories of Bible stories she had heard in church stayed with her, and she knew that even in the worst of times there was a God in heaven who loved her. She wanted so much to be worthy of Him.

"Dear God," she prayed. "Please let me always stay near You. Please help me never do anything that will make me go to hell. Please let me hear Your voice. And if I get too far away from You, please pull me back."

In the evening, the family would sit on the small front porch and talk. William's big voice would roll with laughter. It was infectious, and the children loved to see his jolly face. He looked with affection at his wife Evelyn, encouraging her to relax and come out of the shell in which she had retreated during the hard times. After a while, she grew more cheerful and seemed very pleased when she became pregnant with her first child with William. In the next years, Evelyn gave birth to two other children, Sammy and Laura. Now there were six children in all.

William worked as a cook near the foggy village of Parkdale in a cafe owned by his parents. Parkdale was a typical small town with one gas station and one grocery store. There was a dance hall type establishment with a bar and pool hall, a clean business for working people. William would take the children down to eat ice cream while he played a few games.

Many times, when household noise and pressures grew too much for Evelyn, Shirley and Irene would accompany William to work. They would sit in a tall green cafe booth, play with toys, and eat candy bars.

Irene felt a warm glow in these happy days. She was impressed by his desire to never leave the children unattended. It did not bypass her attention that this was a new kind of love. She felt more comfortable, and the pain and fear of abandonment from long nights sleeping in the closet in Hood River faded. Many evenings Irene and Shirley drifted peacefully into sleep on thick cushions in the cubicle.

On warm summer afternoons, the children wandered across wheat field towards the hull of an old abandoned fishing boat. Nothing remained of the original wood, but the metal superstructure had endured, stretching about 20 feet from end to end and 10 feet sideways. It had been a big old craft and capable of hard work against the mighty winds and waves of the sea. One mast still stood tall, a final sentry holding strong against the elements.

The boat sat on the ground, and Shirley, Irene, or Mike would jump aboard one exposed rib and begin to rock the boat. The other kids clambered aboard, holding tight as the structure swayed from side to side.

"Oh captain, my captain," they would cry. "Where do we sail today?" And so they sailed for the Orient, or across a stormy English Channel, or to an island paradise with lots of food for everyone. Some days they would wear paper hats and play pirates, foraging the high seas for treasure.

They spent days tying ropes to young alder trees, fastening them and then waiting for the trees to remain bent. Then the children would return to ride the curved trees like horses. They played "Lone Ranger" and "Tonto" or "Cowboys and Indians" or a dozen other games created in their child-like imaginations.

When the inevitable childhood injury occurred, hospitals were out of the question. Summer shoes were scarce, so they went barefoot. In the middle of the field, near the rocking boat was an area where canning jars were discarded, their jagged edges hidden in the tall, uncut grass. Irene bounded across the field, stepping squarely on the knife-like edge of a mason jar, cutting three of her toes to the bone. She shrieked for help, crashing to the ground and holding on to the dangling skin and flesh. Soon her brothers and sisters ran to her aid, helping her back to the house. Evelyn took a quick look at the damage, sent Mike running for Winifred, and fainted dead away as she tried to wrap a tight cloth around the foot to slow the bleeding.

Grandma quickly arrived with gauze, scissors, disinfectant, and a needle and thread. She tried to calm Irene, holding her briefly, then, pouring disinfectant on the open wound. She instructed Shirley and Mike to sit on Irene, who screamed and writhed to escape the pain. Winifred began the long ordeal of sewing the bleeding toes back into position. There was no anesthesia, and Irene screamed and wailed. The sewing seemed to take forever. When Winifred completed her stitching, she wrapped Irene's foot tightly in a bandage.

The bandage remained untouched on her foot for several days while she laid on the couch resting. The dressing was never changed, but miraculously no infection took hold. Eventually Irene pestered her mother to remove the bandage to see if she still had toes. Incredibly, her foot was perfectly fine. As she pulled out her own stitches Irene felt strongly that the Lord had protected her foot and prevented dangerous infection.

Another time, William's brother, Uncle Lyle, came with his children for the weekend. The children, all near the same ages, were up at Grandma Winifred's house playing tag and having a wonderful time. Irene tripped in the wet grass, striking her head on a sharp lava rock and ripping part of her ear. Blood poured out from her torn scalp and ear.

Once again Winifred got out her trusty old needle and sewed on Irene's ear. Irene went to school with a huge white gauze bandage covering her head. She was mortified, anticipating the teasing of the school children.

On another occasion, Evelyn lost her temper with Irene. She was playing with her younger sister, and Evelyn wanted the children to put socks on their feet. Irene continued to play with Laura in her walker, not immediately responding to her mother's insistent request. Suddenly Evelyn lost her temper and slugged Irene with her closed fist.

Irene flew across the room, hitting her head on the wooden rocking chair, and splitting open her scalp. She didn't get up. Evelyn took her to the emergency room. The hospital personnel put seven stitches in the gash. Although she was diagnosed with a severe concussion, Evelyn would not allow her to stay in the hospital. No one asked how the concussion had happened.

When food was short Evelyn would choose one or two of the children and take them fishing at Evan's Creek. They would get up before daylight, sometimes packing a lunch, but more often catching fresh fish to eat for breakfast. These were fun occasions, but they also provided fish for the family.

One of Irene's fondest memories of her mother occurred during one of the fishing trips. It was springtime and the water flowed rapidly with the runoff. Irene stepped in too far and fell into the raging torrent. She screamed with fright and Evelyn turned just in time to catch her by the boot straps as she was swept into the current. She pulled Irene into her arms and carried her back to shore. Evelyn held her tight as tears ran down her face.

"Oh sweetie, I love you. Are you all right?" She cried. She pulled Irene's long dark hair back from her face and wiped the water from her eyes. "Oh honey, I don't know what I would do if I ever lost you."

Irene clung to her mother, crying, and hearing for the first time the words she had longed for. They embraced for long moments until they were both calmer. Then with loving hands Evelyn removed Irene's soaking t-shirt and replaced it with her own relatively dry shirt. Long after, Irene would remember the clear message that her mother loved her.

They grew a large garden, nearly an entire acre, which they sharecropped with the grandparents. On summer evenings the family would gather outside to hoe and weed and sing with Evelyn as she exhausted her repertoire of Gershwin songs. They grew corn, beans, potatoes, tomatoes, and other fresh vegetables, along with local fruits to can as foodstuffs through the long winter months. Their voices would ring across the valley as they sang:

Oh we ain't got a barrel of money.
Maybe we're ragged and funny.

But we're traveling along, singing a song,
Side by side.

Evelyn would serenade them with "Summertime" and "Stormy Weather." They would sing until the sun lowered slowly behind the green Oregon hillside. And the times seemed good.

In the summer, William's brother Lyle would come and pick up the children for their annual trip to his farm. Lyle was a fine Christian man and an elder in his church. He showed great generosity to the children. They rode his horses, made homemade ice cream, and had bonfires with hot dogs. It was the youngsters' first introduction to normal family life.

Uncle Lyle would sit and talk to them and read from the Bible and pray for the children. On Sunday he took them all to church. His faith was so genuine, so grounded in a sincere love and belief in Jesus Christ, that Irene grew stronger in her convictions. She loved those summers with Uncle Lyle.

When they returned, Uncle Lyle arranged with the pastor of the Assembly of God church near Parkdale to pick up the children each Sunday and take them to church. He did not want to influence the children away from the church they had attended in Hood River.

Each Sunday morning, the pastor drove out to pick up the kids for Sunday School. He talked to the children about the baptism in the Holy Spirit. Irene was enthralled and longed for her own baptism so she could feel closer to God and have a new way to talk to Him. She thought that He would be able to hear her better if she had a prayer language.

One afternoon on the back porch of the old house she asked the Lord to baptize her in the Holy Spirit. As she sat for a while, looking up at the huge cherry tree which wrapped itself against the house, her heart suddenly filled with a warm glow that she had never experienced.

Tears filled her eyes and she felt the presence of the Lord, as if He were sitting right next to her, His arms embracing her with fatherly love. She opened her mouth and strange words poured out. She felt that a line had opened directly to the throne room of God in heaven. It was wonderful and peaceful and lovely.

After a few minutes she looked around, amazed at what had

transpired. The teaching she had received in church had not explained what came next. And she thought that only adults could have a real and deep relationship with Jesus. As doubts formed in her mind she heard a clear voice say, "You don't want this. This language is from the devil."

She caught her breath with fear. What had she done? She quickly prayed to God and promised not to speak the language again. And so on that porch her prayer language was quenched, and she left behind the new potential in it for a peaceful heart and closeness with God.

At home, the birth of William, Jr., called Willy, increased the financial pressure. Eventually the cafe in Parkdale closed and William, Sr. was forced to look for work away from his family. Evelyn grew fearful about being left alone with all the domestic responsibilities, but they could see no other option. Money was very tight.

William secured work as a commercial fisherman on a boat which launched from Astoria, Oregon, about 150 miles away on the coast. Fishing required that he be aboard the boat for varying periods of time. Many of the trips were only for a day, but his boat also took extended voyages to work the frigid waters off the Alaskan coast. These expeditions lasted for up to two months.

William and Evelyn decided to keep the family in their present home, not wanting to replant the children and feeling a certain security in being close to William's parents. Unknown to William, this decision provided the roots of the complete devastation for his family.

Another child, Sammy, was born — and the family settled into the difficult situation of life without William. Gone was the rollicking laughter and the solid support for Evelyn's fearful nature. She gradually grew bitter and lonely for adult company. The children became accustomed again to beatings for committing the smallest infraction. Pressure and tension colored their existence.

Evelyn was a perfectionist. She would often berate the children for not completing a task to her exacting specifications. "If you can't do it right, then don't do it at all," she would say, then batter the children for their offense. They constantly apologized for doing something wrong, saying "I'm sorry, I'm sorry," over and over, whether they understood their mistake or not.

Evelyn was under tremendous stress, not having enough food or clothing for the children. They were often without shoes, saving their one pair to wear to school. This pair was usually lined with cardboard to cover the holes. In winter the children had no coats or gloves. They wore socks over their hands as mittens and stood huddled together at the bus stop, shielding one another against the cold wind. Irene had only two dresses for school, and often the children had no underwear. This scene provided endless fuel for ridicule from the other students.

The old farm house had no insulation, and many of the windows had no glass. In winter William covered these openings with old cardboard boxes in a vain attempt to block out the frigid weather. Evelyn would take old fashioned clothing irons — the type that are warmed on a wood stove and heated red hot — and would wrap the irons in towels and put them in the bottom of the bed to keep the children warm in the wintry night.

The family received government commodities which stretched their supplies. They received powdered milk, powdered potatoes, peanut butter, and wheat cereal. They used these to stretch the potatoes grown locally and again, learned to live on a meager thin potato soup. There were also endless days of beans, cooked with no meat flavoring. But even this bland diet was better than the days of no food at all in Alaska and Hood River.

Many nights, after bedtime, Evelyn sewed clothes for the children. Then she would sleep late into the morning. When William was gone, the children went to school without breakfast. Days spent at home, they had to wait until she rose to eat anything. If their hunger overcame their fear of punishment they sneaked into the kitchen and raided the peanut butter jar. But Evelyn kept a mental measurement of the amount in the jar. When she got up late in the morning, she would check to see if the children had gotten into the food.

She always caught them. She ordered the children to stand in line, oldest to youngest, while she tried to figure out the guilty party. Often a child would take the punishment for one of the other youngsters. They protected each other in this way. The correction was swift and violent. She used the leaded ropes from William's fishing net and would beat the offender on the back or the back of the legs until blood ran down in rivulets. The children stood stiffly in line, watching in mute terror, waiting until the outrage ended, then held and comforted their injured sibling.

Irene's trust in her mother's good will slowly dissolved as these repeated tirades persisted. Her faith in the favor of other people continued, but she was beginning to learn essential lessons in self preservation. Many of these lessons came hard.

The road from Mount Hood to Portland ran in front of both houses, crossing with another main road just past Grandpa Jess' home. The school bus passed William's house each day, making a left turn on the cross road and stopping parallel with Grandpa Jess' back porch. School children spilled out of the large yellow vehicle dispersing themselves towards homes scattered around the cross road area. There was a worn path lined with lilac bushes which ran from the road straight past Grandpa Jess' back porch and continued across the field to Irene's house.

One afternoon the bus pulled to a stop, unloading its precious cargo at the back of Grandpa Jess' house. Shirley ran ahead of Irene, calling for her to hurry. But Irene dawdled along, lost in her second grade dreams, enjoying the beauty of the orchard trees. She was in no hurry to face the potential furor if her mother wasn't in a good mood. As she walked toward the back porch of Grandpa Jess' house, she noticed him sitting, watching her.

"Hello, Irene," he said.

There was the strangest look in his eye. She was a little nervous about him, but he was, after all, her grandfather.

"Come up and sit with me," he continued.

"Okay, Grandpa." She obeyed, and they sat for several minutes on the porch.

"Tell you what, Irene. Let's go out and let me show you something in my rock shop."

She felt a bit anxious at this sudden show of attention, her natural defense mechanisms kicking into gear. He had never before singled her out in any way from the other children. Then as she thought about it, she grew a little excited, overriding her warning system. Her heart was still so hungry for affection and approval. She missed Grandpa Ernie so badly and thought that maybe Grandpa Jess would love and care for her as Ernie had.

"Okay, Grandpa." He took her hand and they walked together to the small shed. He unlocked and removed the huge padlock from the door of his private sanctuary, leading her inside. He closed and locked the door behind them.

"Nobody comes in here except me, Irene. This is my personal place where I do all my secret things."

She smiled with enthusiasm, looking around for the treasures he was surely creating with the piles of colorful cut rocks. But Grandpa Jess' secret things had nothing to do with treasures or rocks. As he reached for her she finally realized the serious hazard of her predicament. She kicked and screamed, trying to escape, but the door was bolted tight.

Hours later, he unlocked the door and Irene rushed to escape through the opening. He caught her arm.

"Don't you say a word, girlie. You are an evil and vile little child. This is all your fault. If you tell anybody about this, I'll tell them that you started it. I'll tell them not to believe anything you say ever again."

He looked at her hard, right in her eyes, his foul breath burning against her face, and she believed every word clear to the core of her being.

She stumbled across the field toward home, her stomach churning with nausea and fear. As she neared the house, she saw her mother through the kitchen window, tilted-open to catch the occasional breeze. She heard her ranting voice shrieking at one of the children so she went around to the front of the house, settling on the porch and called out for her cat.

"Snowball. Here Snowball," she cried softly into the wind, hoping her mother wouldn't hear. Her voice still choked with emotion. The cat poked its head through the thick growth of wheat in the field beyond her house. The wild animal carefully inspected the area for signs of other human occupation. He would only come when Irene was alone.

And then he was there in her lap, reaching up to lick her face, his rough tongue wiping away her flowing tears.

"What am I going to do now, Snowball?" she asked. "Just what am I going to do?"

I Cry

I remember when I was a little girl.
I had a cat named Snowball.
He was the only friend I had.
Snowball didn't like nobody but me.
But my cat died and I was alone.
And I cried.

I look all around for a friend.
Shirley, will you be my friend?
All she said was go away or I will hit you.
I left her alone but she hit me anyway.
And I cried.

Mama, don't you like me?
I sorry I'm not as good as Shirley.
But I'm trying. I'll do the dishes,
  or clean the house,
But mama please love me . . .
All right mama, I'll leave you alone.
And I cried.

Doesn't anybody care? I care.
All I want is a friend.
All I want is someone to love me . . .
No one answered.
And I cried.

Irene Taylor, age 12

*Hear, O Lord, when I cry aloud; have mercy and be
gracious to me and answer me!*

Psalm 27:7-11 AMP

Irene had already experienced difficulty in school. She was
excellent at repeating stories or information given by her teachers in verbal form. But she could not begin to comprehend the
written word. She could not differentiate between her left and
right, and would often invert letters, such as "E." To Irene, all the

tall straight letters looked the same and all the small round letters appeared identical. She simply could not perceive differences in the letters; therefore, she could not read.

This provided tremendous frustration for her teachers. On the one hand, she had a clear and vivid retention of information given verbally, but the written word was a complete mystery to her. Unfortunately, her instructors did not discover the nature of why she could learn some material so thoroughly while other information completely bypassed her understanding.

Irene felt disapproval from her teachers. She wanted so much to tell someone about the continuing abuse both from her grandfather and her mother, but every adult around seemed angry with her. There was no one she could trust.

On the ride home each evening, she would beg to be let off right in front of her house, rather than having the bus continue on to its scheduled stop near Jess' back porch. Some days the driver would give in and let the children off at home. But most days she would continue on around the corner near the dreaded porch.

At times, Irene would walk the long way around to the front of Jess' house, going along the highway to her house to avoid her grandfather. But Evelyn did not approve of this course, as it kept the children near the mountain traffic, heavy with logging trucks. She could take this long way and face a beating if her mother caught her, or take the trail behind the houses and pray fervently that her grandpa would not be waiting.

It was during these difficult times that Irene's faith was challenged. As she sat on the front porch one evening pouring out her troubles to the Lord she asked, "Why, Jesus? Why?" The tears poured down her young face. "Not everybody has to go through these horrible things. Not everybody's grandpa is so nasty. Why are you letting this happen to me?"

She listened intently in the silence.

"Are you real? Do you even care?" Her heart sank lower and she began to doubt the powerful influence she had felt so long ago. "Maybe I only made You up in my mind. Maybe You're just one of my stories." She stared up at the cherry tree where she often climbed to escape.

Suddenly the sun broke through the clouds. Her mind was

filled with new thoughts, infiltrating and soothing her troubled spirit. She felt a powerful comforting influence like strong arms reaching down from the very gates of heaven to hold her close. And then a voice began to sing, softly, in her head:

> *Farther along we'll know all about it.*
> *Farther along we'll understand why.*
> *Cheer up my brother, walk in the sunlight,*
> *We'll understand it all, by and by.*

It was amazing. No answer was given, no explanation offered, yet the sense of peace was almost overwhelming. She cried again, this time soaking her shirt with liquid gladness. Her spirit was healed for the time, and her unflagging sense of hope renewed.

The situation of repeated abuse from her grandfather and mother, however, did change Irene's personality. She developed a victim mentality, an expectation, almost an anticipation that she would be wounded by the people around her.

There was a spiritual side to this apprehension. It was as if some demonic spirit clasped his claw into her back, and, finding this foothold, would call to other evil authorities to join him. It was a corrupting cycle that influenced her emotions. This cycle produced an unthinkable result, at times pushing Irene to seek the very punishment that her innocent spirit would have avoided.

The summer after second grade, Irene and the kids went to visit Grandpa Ernie and Ada, where they would pick cucumbers and earn a small amount of spending money. The work was not particularly difficult, but took long hours in the large garden area. As the days grew long the children would wander off, speaking to other groups of pickers, playing with the dogs and cats, and meandering in the warm summer sun.

Irene did not like to pick cucumbers because the spiky vines would cut her childish hands — so she spent most of her time pursuing alternative activities. She tried to find other children to play with, but they were mostly occupied. She wandered far from her grandparents, through the orchard groves and toward the farm sheds that protected the machinery. She was befriended by an old Black man, and she would sit talking with him for hours while the others worked. She felt at home with him, but her defense mechanisms were out of order.

One afternoon her friend was not around, and she wandered farther away from her family. She rounded a corner and was confronted by a new man, one she had not seen before. In her loneliness and innate friendliness, she spoke with the man. He told her he was the boss' brother, and he wanted to show her something in the shed.

The man reached for Irene's arm, and she instinctively tried to draw away. But he clasped her firmly, hurting her, and pulled her into the shed.

"Come in here, little girl," he said, and suddenly memories of her ordeals with Grandpa Jess flooded her mind.

"No! Let me go!"

His fingers dug deeper into her thin arm. He drew her across the room toward the high stacked bales of hay.

She screamed and hollered, fighting with all her might. Then from outside she heard another voice yelling for the man.

"You stay here. I'll be right back," he said fiercely, daring her to disobey. He walked out of the opening toward the man hollering his name.

In an instant she was out the door, running quickly away from the voices. She could not run towards her family, as she would have to pass the two men. She searched for a safe place to hide. Outside the barn were piles of cardboard boxes and crates. A small voice in her mind said, "Go in there and hide!"

"Okay, Jesus," she said, recognizing the shelter. She clambered into a large appliance box and pulled the lid down tight. She held her breath as the man's voice came again from around the corner.

"Little girl, little girl. Where are you? Come here!"

She heard the man begin to search through the boxes, banging them and kicking in the sides. He sounded angry. He came closer and closer.

Silently, she prayed with all her might, "Dear Jesus, help me! Please help me — now!"

She heard him come straight for her hiding place. He kicked at her box, his boot denting in the side. She held her hand over her mouth to stifle a scream. Again he kicked at the box, yelling for her, but he never opened the lid. Then his brother came around the barn, called to the man, and he went away.

Irene stayed in the box for a long silent time, wondering if he still waited for her outside. But eventually she eased off the lid and peeked around. She came out of her hiding place and tiptoed to the corner of the barn. The boss stood in the open area, hands on hips, looking for something.

"Oh, there you are," he said kindly. "Are you okay, honey? Did he hurt you?"

"No, I'm okay," she said timidly.

"Well, I'm glad of that." He heaved a sigh of relief. "You stay away from that guy. He is a very bad man."

"Okay," she answered. Then she ran back to her grandparents, thanking Jesus with her every breath.

The longer William was gone, the greater the pressure grew on Evelyn. Her temper grew short with frustration and her patience had long ago dissipated. William toiled in his long and heavy labor aboard the boats and came home to Evelyn's anger and disappointment. Many times the boat caught too few fish and even after hours and days of backbreaking drudgery he came home with only a few dollars. The growing adversity of daily life wore on him.

Eventually William's growing discouragement turned to anger. He joined Evelyn in her rage, and took to beating the children with a heavy belt. Evelyn's weapons were the ropes used on the ship to sink the fish nets. The ropes had lead weights entwined in the rope to weigh them down and to carry the nets deep into icy waters. The children went to school day after day with deep scabbed wounds from being beaten with the lead ropes, the heavy belt or metal clothes hangers.

Amazingly, the school officials did nothing to investigate this obvious abuse. It was common knowledge that all of this family's children bore these marks, evidence of the blood battles woven into the fabric of their family life. One teacher did attempt to ask Evelyn about the scars on her children, and was told to shut up and mind her own business. The teacher did just that.

The children still played and acted, for the most part, as if nothing unusual was happening. Irene continued on in school, struggling to learn to read and trying with super-human effort to understand concepts she felt were just beyond her reach. She was able to do math, as the rules were simpler, more concrete, and she could read numbers much easier than she could read letters. God enabled Irene to memorize scripture verses. Although she had great difficulty reading the Bible, she could quickly commit to memory things other people read to her or said out loud. She memorized the Twenty-third Psalm and would sit on the front stoop saying it over and over, thinking that there was really a God who loved and cared for her.

Irene was also left handed, a "condition" defined in the 1958 edition of Webster's Dictionary as meaning "like an imbecile." Her teachers fought in vain to force her to use her right hand.

She tried very hard to please everybody. At school she made every attempt to read and write properly. And at home she tried to satisfy her mother by cleaning the house, cooking meals (even as a very small child), and doing everything "right." Yet her mother would emerge from her own pit of unhappiness to berate the child: "You stupid fool. Can't you do anything right?" or "You are just a clumsy slew-foot!" or "I guess you're just the Ugly Duckling, Irene."

Irene lived in mortal terror of doing something wrong. At one point, the school officials decided that Irene must be retarded in some way. During an occasional visit from Grandpa Ernie and Grandma Ada, Irene was scheduled to be tested at a nearby institution for the mentally disabled. She was frightened, as her mother had not so gently warned her of what was to happen. She thought that they were testing to see if she was crazy, or at least like one of those people she saw drooling behind the tall iron gates. Her horror almost paralyzed her as she got into the car to be taken to the institution. As they started the car, Grandpa Ernie ran out and stopped them. He opened the door and threw his arms around her saying, "Irene, you're going to be just fine. You just go take that test and do your very best. Remember, you're a very smart little girl, and you'll always be that way to me." Irene looked up at him with tear-filled eyes, and then they went to take the test.

Because Irene was only in second grade, the IQ test that was chosen was almost totally verbal. The monitor read each question to Irene aloud, and Irene could give the answer orally. She had to read and write only a small portion of the test. It was a breeze. Her IQ was measured above 160, much to the dismay of

53

her teachers and parents.

But this accomplishment almost immediately backfired. She was so thrilled to have done well, to have pleased her parents and especially Grandpa Ernie, that it never occurred to her how their expectations for her would change. Now she was branded an underachiever. She obviously wasn't working to her full potential or trying hard enough.

In a matter of weeks her mother wrote a strong note to her school teacher, showing the note to Irene first. It said, "Irene is just lazy and doesn't know how to do anything. If you need to spank her at school, you just spank her. Make her do her work correctly, using any means you please."

The teacher complied vehemently with the request, striking Irene over and over with a ruler across the knuckles when she made a mistake in reading or writing. At home she was beaten repeatedly and with great force for every bad grade on her report cards.

Irene became very angry at this. Her little girl temper wanted to strike out at something. She tried very hard, especially at handwriting, forming her letters slowly, forcing against the upside-down style of many left-handed people, endeavoring to be perfect. Her teacher said that left-handed people always wrote at a strange slant and ran over the lines. Irene practiced for hours to perfect her penmanship, but still got her knuckles cracked with the ruler.

The message rapidly got to Irene's classmates that she was not quick to read or reply to questions. She was often set up as the butt of their cruel jokes. When the teacher asked for volunteers to read aloud in class her name was offered by numerous pupils. She would try to beg off, and then would have to stumble through the oral assignment, only to become the subject of their endless jibes: "Stupid girl! She can't even read 'Dick and Jane' books!" or "Retard!" or "Bug-eyes!" Irene tried in vain to make friends, but these derisive names kept the other children at arm's length. Who wanted to befriend a "retard"?

The only real appreciation Irene received as a child was for her singing. Even Evelyn would shower her with praise when she sang. She never criticized as Irene performed a new song for her. It seemed to raise Evelyn's spirits, and she often insisted that Irene sing for guests.

Irene was a quick study, learning and playing most of the songs from memory as she had first with her mother in Alaska and later with Grandpa Ernie. In this area she finally experienced her first and only success. She sang in little plays at school and in church during the summer with Uncle Lyle. Her voice had a strong, pure quality, capable of landing with soft accuracy on the highest notes.

Her singing gave great pleasure to the people around her and provided positive recognition for her as a person. Music allowed her to escape, to hide in some imaginary world where she was in control of all aspects of her reality. In music everything was beautiful and harmonious.

She wrote short poems and songs about funny little animals or beautiful flowers. With music she was no longer that little ugly girl, the one who was forced to visit her grandpa in his rock shop, day after day. She could escape the child she saw in her own mind, the one that was such a nuisance to everyone, the ugly duckling always in trouble. In music she could be a fairy princess, a lovely lady, a whole person appreciated for her every word and deed — and of course, a person totally accepted and loved.

In winter the trees shimmered with frost. When the wind blew, the trees shone with rainbow iridescence, like little specks of diamonds all over the branches. Irene would look out the window to see the moon rise in late evening, watching its light transform the old cherry tree standing just outside her window.

In summer she would climb high into the tree to avoid some expected punishment. It was a protected place. She would sometimes sit up there all day long, knowing she was in trouble, but that the tree was out of Evelyn's reach. In winter she could not scale the slick bark, but gazed at it longingly, remembering the promise of safety that would return in spring.

As winter arrived, the house grew colder both spiritually and physically. The children gathered on the enclosed porch each morning, dressing near the wood stove for warmth. They dressed quietly, leaving Evelyn to sleep in.

The children missed William enormously when he was gone. If he was expected home on a particular day, Irene would trudge up the steep slope of the nearest high hill and plant herself on a rock. She would search the horizon for hours looking for the familiar green Chevy flatbed to pull over the far hill and chug down the road toward home. Often on his return William brought presents, surprises that the children cherished. He brought skates, or stuffed toys, or dolls, or Tonka trucks. But more often money was so tight that the treasures were provisions to replenish a larder empty of even a rotten potato.

When William was home, he cooked breakfast for them: pancakes stacked high on top of hot bacon. He helped the children get ready for school, and periodically tried to get Evelyn to take more responsibility in caring for them. These discussions always led to Evelyn screaming at William and his retreat into a quizzical silence. He would not fight her. He loved her very much, but he could not understand why she would not care for her children.

As financial pressures closed in, Evelyn retreated farther and farther into some unreachable space, coming out only to rage and beat the children. She began to drink in secret, fearful of William's parents, but needing the escape more.

Soon spring crept across the landscape, evidenced by the blooming of thousands of apple and plum trees. Irene's spirits lifted. She and the other children would play in the wheat grass field, laying for hours looking up at imaginary cloud shapes. Sometimes she wanted to share her private hell with a brother or sister, but she always held back, feeling an overwhelming guilt about her participation in her grandfather's filthy games. She was sure that, in some way, it must be all her fault. So she kept her silence, not noticing in her self absorption the strange quiet of her brothers and sisters.

She wondered about Grandma Winifred. Did she know about Jess? How could these unthinkable things happen in the midst of all these people without anybody suspecting? But even her child mind could imagine Winifred's fear of rejection, the loss of her husband, and the public disgrace. Irene was very familiar with these fears. And so it remained a humiliating secret.

By now there were six children sharing one of the two bedrooms in William's home. At first Shirley, Irene, Mike, and Willy shared one double bed. It was an uncomfortable situation as the younger children were not entirely potty trained. Some nights the children woke up soaking wet, but had no other place to sleep. When Sammy and Laura came along, a bunk bed was added to the crowded little room.

When fishing season slowed down, around November, William cut Christmas trees to sell in Portland. Nine years old and in the fourth grade now, Irene was able to assist with this physical work, and he hired her to help. This was her first opportunity to earn money. William would take a logging truck into the woods to cut the trees, then dump them in the front yard of the house. Irene stood up high in the flatbed truck and caught the trees as he handed or threw them to her.

At the end of Christmas season, Irene received $15 for her work. William smiled at her joy in collecting these rare funds.

"What are you going to do with all that money, Irene?" he asked.

"I'm going to buy me a coat, Dad."

She glowed with anticipation, not noticing the look of guilt that passed quickly over his face.

"Okay, let's go to town," he said, opening the truck door.

She led him into the only store in Parkdale which carried children's clothing. She looked over several garments and finally settled on a beautiful bright blue car coat with clean white fuzzy fur lining the hood. To Irene it was exquisite. It was also the first coat she had ever owned in her whole life.

When Irene turned 10 years old, just before fifth grade, her mother was seriously injured in a car wreck, breaking her back in four places. William arranged with Uncle Lyle to watch the children during her absence. Although the children were anxious about their mother's condition, they were overjoyed to stay with their uncle. For months they stayed on the farm, basking in the healthy environment. There was warm sunshine, clean clothing, and plenty to eat.

After the years of abuse and spiritual deprivation, this extended stay with Uncle Lyle's fine family awakened in Irene a growing desire to know more about Jesus, to have His comfort, and to be able to count on Him for help in her difficulties.

They attended church regularly and were taught more about a God who cared for them. Irene prayed for her parents, "Please save my mom and dad." And in a miracle of faith, she even prayed for her degenerate grandfather, "And please help Grandpa Jess."

She watched the people singing and worshipping the Lord and thought how wonderful it all was. How clean and peaceful and holy life could be. As she watched the people leading the service, somehow she knew that some day she would stand up in front and lead people in praising Almighty God. She gained courage for the future and confidence that her life wouldn't always be such a mess.

During the summer of Irene's fifth grade year, she became aware of a new strain in the household. She could feel the storm clouds gathering over the family. One afternoon she watched surreptitiously as Shirley talked in tense whispering tones to her mother. Evelyn's jaw tightening as she questioned Shirley closely. Then William was called in. He listened intently to Evelyn, then interrogated Shirley.

Irene crept closer to hear the conversation and decided in her young mind that the subject concerned Grandpa Jess and Shirley. She thought that the time had come for her to step forward. She walked into the room.

"Dad, I want to tell you something." William swung around and frowned at her.

"Not now, Irene;" he brushed her off.

"But, Dad, it isn't just Shirley. . . ." He cut her off.

"I don't care. It's none of your business. I don't want to hear those kind of stories." Irene shrank back out of the room, stung with the realization that only Shirley's pain and humiliation was believed by her parents. They wouldn't even listen to her. It did not occur to her that she could be mistaken about the conversation, which was actually an argument started by Shirley's irritation with the lack of space and privacy.

The family conference lasted into the night, with voices rising in anger, then falling into low anxious whispers. By morning it was settled. The family would move to Astoria. No specific reason was given to the children, except that William wanted Shirley to have her own bedroom.

Irene boiled with anger, thinking that they cared only about Shirley and her problems. At least the move would mean having William at home much more of the time.

ASTORIA

Why was I not stillborn? Why did I not give up the ghost when my mother bore me? Why did thy knees receive me? Or why the breasts, that I should suck? For then should I have lain down and been quiet; I should have slept; then had I been at rest [in death], With kings and counselors of the earth, who built up [now] desolate ruins for themselves; Or with princes who had gold, who filled their houses with silver. Or [why] was I not a miscarriage, hidden and put away, as infants who never saw light. There [in death] the wicked cease from troubling, and there the weary are at rest. **There the [captive] prisoners rest together; they hear not the taskmaster's voice.** *The small and the great are there, and the servant is free from his master. Why is light [of life] given to him who is in misery, and life to the bitter in soul, Who long and wait for death, but it comes not, and dig for it more than for hid treasures; Who rejoice exceedingly, and are elated when they find the grave? [Why is the light of day given] to a man whose way is hidden, and whom God has hedged in? For my sighing comes before my food, and my groanings are poured out like water.* **For the thing which I greatly fear comes upon me, and that of which I am afraid befalls me.** *I was not or am not at ease, nor had I or have I rest,* nor was I or am I quiet, yet trouble came and still comes upon me.

Job 3:11-26 AMP

"How much longer, Irene?" Mike asked, peering over the top of the truck cab, his face feeling stiff in the blowing cold wind.

"How should I know, Mike?" she answered, poking her head up against the gust. "I've never been to Astoria before."

Shirley, Irene, Mike, and Willy huddled against the brisk air under a green tarp in the back of William's old army truck. Tall slats on either side held the wind at bay until curiosity motivated the children to stand on a crate behind the cab to look out over the front. After a few minutes, with their faces in the strong wind, they would run back and dive under the tarp, peering out the back of the truck.

Their excitement was overwhelming. Astoria seemed like heaven to them. Evelyn had talked for days about the potential of their new lives, how they would have a nice huge house. Each child would have his own room and private bed. William would be able to come home most evenings, and they would be like a real family. Evelyn was thrilled to be living in town again, to be able to do things and go places with other people.

In the four-hour drive from Parkdale to Astoria, Irene had ample time to think about the many implications concerning the move. With her dad home, perhaps her mom would be happier, less irritable and violent with the children. The larger house would place less strain on the whole family. Everybody would have more privacy and more space just to live. Each child would have his own bed — no more waking up soaking wet from some sibling's nighttime accident.

What made all this sink into an irrelevant oblivion was that there would be no more Grandpa Jess. No more aching, sweating, white-faced tension, waiting to see if the bus would let her off at home or take her on beyond the loathsome back porch. No more soul-wrenching guilt over thinking that everything that happened was her own fault.

She was so sure that nothing could ever happen again to approach how horrible life had been in Parkdale. She looked once again over the cab, hardly containing her anticipation of life in Astoria. She had never known such joy and hope.

And once again, as in the past, her emotions were so strong and jumbled that she did not notice similar sentiments in the faces of her brothers and sisters.

As the truck approached the bridge crossing the Columbia River from Warrenton to Astoria, the children all stood up to catch the first vision of their new home.

"There it is, kids!" William yelled out the open window. "Isn't it beautiful?" They all shouted and hugged each other, jumping up and down on the wood floor of the old truck.

He drove on through town, pointing out the Astor Column, the sandstone monument marking the end of the Oregon Trail. Even in the chilly fall weather, evidence of the masses of blooming foliage still remained. They rode by the river docks, astonishing the children with the hundreds of colorful boats tied against the piers. William pointed out his bright blue fishing boat. It was the first time the family had seen it.

He parked the truck at the dead end on 29th Street, and they piled out, following him excitedly up the alley way to their new home. A profusion of lilac bushes screened the daylight basement from view. The children clambered up the plank sidewalk to the long narrow porch that lined the front of the enormous old house.

Inside, the dining room had a tall ceiling covered with Victorian tiles made of aluminum painted white. The floors were constructed of oak, but had never been finished, and they sagged. There were no rugs or insulation to prevent the cold from seeping up from the chilly basement. The abandoned bordello, probably built in the 1870s, had been repossessed for taxes, and William got it for $400. It was 1963.

The lower part of the walls were dark oak panels with wainscoting up high. And the walls above were covered with faded green and yellow wallpaper, decorated with dancing ladies in Victorian dress. The windows had old-fashioned lead panes that shone like prisms in the light. There was a large, old, round oak table with claw feet. The table had ample room for the whole family, but there were only two chairs. There was a dilapidated couch with a green vinyl cover. High on the wainscoting was a built-in shelf where treasures could stay out of the reach of tiny hands.

William led the family on a tour of their new home, through the kitchen with its new stove and brand-new washer and dryer. The kitchen area had no cupboards or storage and had probably been a parlor, but with the addition of the stove it served the purpose. Next to the kitchen were two bedrooms. William assigned these rooms as he showed the house to his family.

Up the old rickety staircase, on the second floor were five bedrooms along a narrow, dimly lit hallway. William continued his tour by assigning the rooms to each child.

Then they all went downstairs into the basement. The door opened onto a mud-floored room with a path of planks which led across to the rear of the house. There was a small room, almost like an outhouse, which had a toilet with a light bulb hanging down over it and no sink or tub. This was the bathroom.

The house had many pieces of old furniture left by the previous tenants. Each bedroom had an old iron bed and a dresser, but there was only one closet in the entire house. The closet, off the upstairs hallway, was filled with dismantled antiques, legs from this and that chair or table, and broken pieces of belongings long ago forgotten.

The house had an eerie feeling: strange sounds seemed to follow the children, especially late at night. Often they would enter a room and catch a glimpse of a figure in a window that quickly faded. Occasionally blankets and other objects would fly across a room when no one else was near. It was creepy.

The third evening after moving in, Irene started up the stairs to her room and noticed that the single light bulb at the head of the long dark hallway had burnt out. She glanced down to find her footing, then looked back at the head of the staircase. A human figure stood there in the dim light, staring down at her. Then the figure turned and walked down the hall.

Irene screamed and flattened herself against the wall. Then she ran into the kitchen, got a new light bulb, and crept carefully back up the stairs. At the top she peered around the corner down the dark empty hallway. The corridor was empty. She stood on tiptoe to replace the light. Suddenly she felt hands grab her around the waist and push her across the landing and down the staircase. She tumbled down the steep stairs without serious injury and in extreme fright she looked back up. No one was there.

Later neighbors told them that at least three people had been murdered in the house, and it was notorious throughout Astoria for strange and mysterious occurrences. The children grew fearful of all sorts of terrifying events, both real and imagined.

Aside from the experience of living in the "haunted" house,

the first year in Astoria was good. Irene had her own bedroom at the top of the stairs with her own bed and dresser. Her father even made a place in the room to hang her clothes. Her room had a window, with glass in it, and a little curtain. Her parents allowed her to paint the room lavender, her favorite color. But most importantly, she had some privacy.

That first year, William did well in the commercial fishing business, and he was usually home with the family. Evelyn grew open and more cheerful. She rarely beat the children. She sang often and seemed to enjoy their good fortune. She and the children had clothes and shoes, with coats for winter.

That Christmas was a very special time. Money was more plentiful than usual. The house seemed warm and special. William cut a gigantic Christmas tree that reached to the top of the high ceiling in the living room. A week before Christmas, he lifted up 11-year-old Irene and allowed her to carefully place the old pipe cleaner angel on the top branch.

The tree was surrounded with piles of presents, more than they ever had before. And Irene received a Bugs Bunny doll with a talking pull string. She cherished this toy and felt that she had finally achieved some measure of approval from her parents.

She took fifth grade over, because of her previous difficulties, but seemed to have more success in her new surroundings. She liked her teachers and received help from them in her difficulties with reading.

But Irene, Mike, Willy, and Laura still experienced complications in their relationships with school children. Once Mike was being picked on by other children, and Irene stepped in. The ruffian involved punched her squarely in the nose, splitting the cartilage and flattening her nose to her face. She was taken to the doctor, who told them she needed plastic surgery to reconstruct the nose. But there was no money for such frivolity. Eventually the nose healed in its new shape.

In the evening, Evelyn and William went down to the Desmona Tavern, leaving Irene to cook and care for the children. This was the lifestyle Evelyn had longed for in her loneliness in Parkdale. As time went on and William took longer trips on the seas, she began going to the bar by herself. As her dependence on alcohol grew more serious, the old behaviors returned.

When the children came home from school, Evelyn would leave Shirley in charge and head down for the bar. Shirley would sit in queenly grandeur on the vinyl couch and give orders to Irene, such as, "Go do the dishes, or I'll beat the living daylights out of you."

"No way. You're not the boss," Irene would say. Then Shirley would slug Irene with all her might.

"Mom said I was in charge. Do what I say, or I'll tell her when she gets home." This threat brought memories of countless beatings, so Irene would obey Shirley. As time went on Irene simply adopted these chores as her lot in life, and she took on the responsibilities of mothering the four younger children.

She cooked meals, washed dishes, tried to keep clean clothes prepared for school, scrubbed the wood floors, as well as performed the other chores. Sometimes the little ones tried to help, but more and more the duties fell on Irene's young shoulders.

Shirley protected herself by filling her mother's ears with a variety of lies and tales about Irene. She would tattle on her and try to get Evelyn to doubt Irene's word. Evelyn still retained that old favoritism for her first born child so it was not hard for her to accept Shirley's version of any incident.

Irene eventually stopped standing up for herself. Her shoulders drew in around her. Her waist-length dark brown hair hung like limp dark ropes down the sides of her face. She was slender beyond what was fashionable or healthy, and she looked older than her 11 years.

Her knowledge of the appropriate relationships between a child and a parent was particularly warped. It never occurred to her that Jesus had anything different in mind for her life. She still prayed and held on to that child-like faith that had kept her from sinking into despair during all those years in Parkdale, but she had no expectations that life could be any different.

Many afternoons she would sneak off to the dock and sit with Puddles dreaming her far off dreams and praying that God would make her a good enough little girl to deserve a better life. These dreams fed her hopes and motivated her to try and make life better for her brothers and sisters.

One afternoon Evelyn sent Irene on an errand to the store, just down the street from their house. She gratefully accepted this assignment to escape the drudgery of housework and be allowed out alone. She walked passed the two taverns and several flop houses, peering cautiously into the mysterious interiors, then proceeded to the grocery store.

She bought a red licorice rope and her mother's groceries, then strolled home, happy to have both the candy and the treat of freedom. She sauntered along not paying particular attention to her surroundings. As she neared the second tavern she became aware of a big car driving slowly up beside her. The car pulled in front of her, turning into the alley and cutting her off on the sidewalk. She stopped and saw a dark-haired man in his late 50s open the car door half-way.

"Do you know how to get to Seaside?" he asked.

"Yeah, you go down this road and you make a left . . . I mean a right," she answered, pointing. Suddenly he grabbed her hand and tried to pull her into the car. He held her tightly by the wrist and reached with his other hand to open his zipper. As he exposed himself to her, she screamed and hit him, yanking herself out of his grasp.

She ran home as fast as she could and, in gasping breaths, told her mother what had happened. To Irene's surprise, Evelyn called the police and reported the incident. Soon black and white cars pulled down the alley as officers came to question Irene. She told them in detail what had happened and gave a clear description of the man. Then the incident was over.

Days later they discovered that the man had molested and murdered two other children earlier that same week. Irene would have been victim number three.

The police caught the man from Irene's description. She picked him out of a lineup, and he was convicted for his crimes.

One day, weeks later, it struck her just what she had escaped. She went up to her room and looked out the window, tears of fear welling up in her eyes.

"Where are you, Jesus? Why do some terrible things happen, then I turn around and you save my life? I don't understand."

As she pondered these incidents, she began to see that even though her life was difficult and frustrating, though horrible damage had been inflicted on her, the Lord still watched over her, still kept her from irrevocable destruction. Deep inside there was

a part of her that remained whole, untouched by any of this devastation. It was the part of her that still walked and talked with
the Lord. In the quietness of her private room, a voice spoke softly
in her mind.

"I love you, Irene. I have always loved you. I will use these
things in the future to help other people, if you let Me. Though
your life will be hard, I'll always be with you." She pondered the
meaning of those words.

"Though your life will be hard, I'll always be with you," the
voice repeated. She lay down in her bed and repeated over and
over a scripture she had learned in church. "The Lord is my Shep-
herd, I shall not want . . ."

William eventually installed a bathtub in the basement near the
front of the house by an uncovered window. Until this time, the
family had made do with sponge baths. The tub sat on planks in
the mud and was filled from a pipe running straight down from
the kitchen. The children were overjoyed with this moderniza-
tion, but quickly learned to stay carefully on the boards. One side
step and the bath had to be repeated to remove the thick oozing
mud. The lilac bushes prevented neighbors from viewing these
daily acrobatics.

William made this and other improvements during his infrequent stays at home. As time went on, he stayed longer on the
boats, following the fish on their migrations up to Alaska. Evelyn
grew lonely again. She would take the children to the roller skating rink and meet young men from the Job Corps. She would
bring them home and have parties. She encouraged Shirley to
flirt with these fellows and would laugh gaily when they would
kiss and fondle her daughter. She thought of this as normal childish fun. The potential consequences did not cross her mind.

Evelyn drank more heavily, spending most of her days inco-
herent from intoxication. Shirley stayed away with her friends or
came home to play "boss." She took no responsibility and was
not forced to perform chores. She clearly took advantage of being the favorite child, but Irene could see that this situation was
not her fault and tried to understand her sister's behavior.

Evelyn would wait for the children to get home from school,
set out the chores, then head down the alley to the Desmona
Tavern. Sometimes she would already be inebriated, sitting at the

kitchen table and crying in heavy sobs about how bad her life was. Other days she would already be gone to the saloon by the time they got home, and Irene would go to the neighbor's house to pick up the pre-schoolers.

The children learned that their mother would behave better if she knew they were bringing home company. They started inviting friends, asking them to dinner and giving Evelyn warning the night before. Shirley would bring home Job Corps boys she had met skating or boys from school, knowing that Evelyn would excavate herself out of her drunken despair, dress, cook dinner, and act like a perfect hostess for their guests. The other children copied this behavior. They learned to play on their mother's pride to protect themselves from her drunken rages.

Except for these occasions, Evelyn was totally dependent on Irene to run the house. She cooked all the meals, cleaned and scrubbed the floors, waxing them to a brilliant shine. The gloss would quickly fade, as the floor had no finish. She came home from school to laundry, chores, and to diaper and feed the younger children. She gave them baths and played with them. She was not allowed to attend parties or activities at school except those which involved music.

If she argued with any of these duties there was the requisite beating with a broom stick, with Evelyn screaming and yelling for Irene to obey her mother. And with her growing victim mentality she was reticent to defy the drunken authority. She came to enjoy, if not the work load, at least the fact that her work prevented the kids from going hungry and their clean clothes gave them more acceptance by their peers at school.

School officials often called Irene, taking her out of class to deal with her brother. Mike had a continual problem with incontinence. He would become upset with some situation at school and wet himself — and at the age of 10, this behavior received little understanding. Day after day, Irene cared for her brother, hovering in embarrassment in the boys' restroom. School officials would question her about what made him do that. She was at a loss to explain Mike's problem. Irene knew that something was wrong, but was not old enough nor did she have enough information to discern this residual effect of the emotional damage inflicted by Grandpa Jess.

Evelyn would berate Mike for humiliating her. She sent extra clothes with him, instructing Irene to take care of it. Sometimes he went to school in clothing still wet from an accident in the night. The teachers sent notes home instructing Evelyn to make sure he was clean before he came to school. All of this mortified Mike. He was lost in a morass of confusion. His body was out of control and his emotions had been viciously damaged.

Eventually, Mike was sent to a Catholic priest for counseling. He went on a regular basis, and later Shirley also attended private counseling sessions with this priest. Irene went only once. She was uncomfortable with the man and had no intention of returning for a second time. The priest made an appointment for her to return for further instruction. But when she returned for her engagement she found the office piled high with boxes of his belongings. He had been arrested for child molestation and had been taken away by the church to a treatment center. Irene wondered about the conversations he had had with her brother Mike.

In sixth grade, Irene asked her father for a flute so she could join her school band. He bought her a nickel plated instrument and made her promise to practice every day and do her very best. She also committed to giving him a concert every time he returned from his ocean voyages.

This flute and her voice provided legitimate excuses for absences from the house. She would go to extra rehearsals with the band. Often she was invited to sing at community functions. Evelyn never minded when Irene attended these events as she took pride in these accomplishments. However, she and William never attended the functions. Her personal shame in the alcoholism and her life style outweighed her desire to see her daughter perform. And she knew deep inside that Irene would be ashamed if she showed up in some stage of intoxication.

Irene's talent with music proved to be a mixed blessing in her relationship with Evelyn. Part of her mother was proud of her accomplishments, her voice and her flute, but another part of her rose up in anger and resentment toward her daughter.

She felt a certain jealousy of Irene's success, along with a resentment of her accomplishments which seemed to, at times, make her outshine Shirley. When Irene was 13, this jealousy developed into a resentment of her personal appearance.

"Irene, come in here!" Evelyn shouted from the kitchen.

"Okay, Mom," Irene complied nervously.

"You spend way too much time combing your hair and brushing your teeth. I don't like it. You are vain about your hair and your teeth." Irene looked at her in dismay.

"What?" she asked.

"You heard me. You are a vain and selfish girl." She paced the room thinking aloud. "I've got to do something about this. Hmm. Okay, let's go down to the beauty parlor, and I'm going to have them cut your hair off."

"No, Mom, please no. I don't want to." Irene's dark hair hung far below her waist and was, in her mind, her only claim to beauty. She could not believe what was happening.

"Let's go, or I'll cut it off myself."

Irene knew there was no recourse.

"Can't Shirley come and get hers cut too?" Irene asked.

"No, she's not as vain about her hair as you are." Evelyn took Irene by the arm and pulled her out of the house and down to the beauty parlor. There the hairdresser sheared her lovely dark brown hair to boyish shortness. Irene was just sick.

Things were beginning to fall apart. Evelyn discovered to her disbelief that she was pregnant with her seventh child. A few months into the pregnancy, she was diagnosed with ovarian cancer. This pressure sent her completely over the edge. She drank every day, all day long. No longer did she make any attempt to hide her consumption of alcohol.

She considered having an abortion, but she could not stand the thought of sacrificing the life of her growing baby for her own convenience.

"My life is not worthy of saving at the expense of this child's life," she told William as they argued over the doctor's advice. "Maybe this baby will grow up and have a better life than mine. How can I take that chance away? How could I be that selfish?"

They fought over the decision. William's fear of losing Evelyn made him adamant that she should have an abortion. And as the months passed, and he became more certain that Evelyn would not survive the pregnancy, he distanced himself from the inevitable pain. But Evelyn knew in her heart that this was the best thing she had ever done in her whole life.

Evelyn sensed William's withdrawal, bitterly feeling his lack of support as the doctors waited impatiently for the baby's birth, unable to render cancer treatment to the pregnant woman. They hoped that her pregnancy hormones would retard the growth of the tumor.

Life at home was hellish. Between the stress of the pregnancy, fear of the cancer and dying, and the endless bottles of beer, Evelyn's moods changed hourly. She still invited men over, both for Shirley and to keep herself company. And again, she promoted promiscuity in her daughters. Irene was disgusted by the whole situation and was not enticed by the kind of men flowing in a steady stream through her house. But Shirley loved the attention.

Ruth was born in February. The following day, Evelyn was rushed for emergency surgery at the University Hospital in Portland. The cancer was successfully removed, and Evelyn stayed in the hospital for two weeks. The new baby was given to kind neighbors for care until Evelyn was released from the hospital.

On the day of their return, William placed the tiny baby in Irene's young arms. Irene would act as mother to the infant for most of her tender years. Evelyn never regained the ability to care for the children.

Five months after Ruth's birth, Evelyn raised herself from a drunken stupor to observe Shirley's ever widening waistline. She rallied herself off the couch and took her oldest "darling" daughter by the arm, shaking her viciously.

"What's this?" she demanded.

"What do you mean, Mom?"

"You know what I mean."

Shirley sneered back at her mother. "It's your fault. You keep those guys coming in here all the time. What did you expect?"

Evelyn slapped her across the face. Shirley looked at her mother, fear pushing back her arrogance.

"It wasn't them, Mom. It was William. He did it. He made me. Please, Mom, get him away from me!" She lied with conviction. Evelyn, shamed by the accusation that this could have been her fault, believed her. It was her influence, inviting countless boys into the house.

She preferred with all her heart to believe that William had molested her daughter. So warped was her affection for her devious offspring and still hurt from his lack of support when she had cancer, she turned against the years of William's affection. Time and time again he had proved his love and support for her, and she threw it all away by believing one great monstrous lie from the mouth of her daughter.

When William returned, all hell broke loose. Evelyn met him at the door and began a rampage that continued for days. She raged at him, accusing him of this and other imagined evils. He told her over and over that he was not guilty, that he had never touched Shirley. He cried tears begging her not to believe the vicious fabrication. He offered to take a lie detector test and went down to the police station and reported the situation. The officials complied with his request and William passed the test with flying colors. The police reported the results to Evelyn.

Finally, after days of endless battle, Evelyn faced the fact that Shirley lied. They sat down at the kitchen table, and Evelyn got the truth out of her. Shirley told her mother which boy she suspected was the father. Then, while William and Evelyn considered what to do, Shirley planned to climb down the huge maple tree that branched out near her bedroom window to run away and elope with the father of her baby.

William learned of the plan from the other children. He went out late one afternoon and cut the tree down. He was determined that even after the cruel treatment he had received from Shirley, he would not allow her to ruin her life by marrying the unacceptable young man. Besides, Shirley was only 15 years old.

William returned to the sea and Evelyn to her drinking, losing herself in stronger rampages against the children. She beat them unmercifully for any small or imagined infraction. Her moods oscillated from extreme happiness and gaiety to intense fury for no reason. The children learned to tiptoe around her, never sure of what would come next.

Irene spent as much time away from her as possible, staying in her room, praying to God for hours to protect her from her mother. She would sit with Puddles at the dock and dream about a better life, about a future in the absence of emotional fireworks. Little by little, her spirit rose with the first pangs of defiance.

One afternoon, she ran with Pud up the plank sidewalk and quietly entered the house. Immediately her mother was on her, chasing her through the house, the broom handle flailing at her head. Irene didn't even know what she had done wrong. As she ran into the kitchen a voice seemed to say, "How long is this going to go on?" She paused for a moment, feeling the blow strike her shoulder.

Then she turned and drew herself up into her mother's face and yelled, "Stop it!"

Evelyn drew a breath of amazement and prepared to strike her again. This time Irene grabbed the broom with both hands and wrenched it forcefully away from her mother.

"You're never going to beat me again," she spoke into the shocked face of her mother. "This is the last time that you will ever hit me. Why don't you just go to hell. You are the sorriest excuse for a mother I have ever seen."

Evelyn stood in total shock as Irene stalked out of the room, taking the broom handle with her.

As she went to her room, she heard Evelyn call to Shirley and Shirley's young husband Jim to go with her to the bar.

"You can go to your room, but you still have to watch the children!" she called up to Irene.

Irene was steaming mad. She went down the hall and got a paper bag from the closet. In it, she placed her two pairs of underwear, a shirt, and one pair of pants. She waited on the landing until her brothers and sisters were all asleep and then she left the house.

She went to a friend's house, called Grandma Ada and asked her to come and get her. She told her that she didn't want to live with her mother any more, that she wanted to come and live at Ada's house. By morning, her grandmother's blue truck pulled up to take her away to peace in Portland.

The next day they called to tell Evelyn what had happened so that she would not worry. But Evelyn was furious that Irene had left — first, because her daughter had showed the strong defiance; second, because her worst fear of losing her children to her parents had been fulfilled. But the strongest reason for her anger was that she now had no one to clean the house and care for the children.

She called the police and gave them some invented story, and the following morning officers arrived at the home of Ernie and

Ada. They introduced themselves and spoke briefly to the grandparents, then explained their presence. As Irene came down the stairs in her nightgown, they grabbed her and started for the door. Ernie shouted at them to at least let her get dressed.

"You damn fools. The least you can do is let her put on clothes. This is the worst thing I've ever seen, the police come just because you go visit your grandparents. Don't you know she gets tired of getting beat up all the time. I wouldn't want to live with that drunken woman either, and she's my own daughter!" They relented and allowed Irene to put her clothes on.

When she came down the stairs, the officers put her in handcuffs and placed her in the back seat of the patrol car and delivered her to juvenile hall in Portland.

Irene walked down the long halls lined with children peering out of their "cells" at her. She took the required shower with the heavy antiseptic shampoo designed for delousing. They took her clothing and gave her a dark gray outfit, a shirt, pants with a tie belt, and some tennis shoes. Then she settled into the routine for the next four or five days.

It wasn't half bad. During the day, the children watched television and did school work. Food was plentiful and good. Their only chores consisted of picking up after themselves and taking care of their own space. Irene thought that if she couldn't stay with her grandparents she could at least remain in this place of peace and safety. But she was soon released and taken back home to Evelyn and William and the creepy old house.

As the inevitability of the situation became clear to Irene, she decided to make the best of it. No matter what she did it was clear that she would never get away, that no one would believe how bad it was in her home.

In a few days, after she got the house back into shape and began to regain her mother's good graces, she asked to take the children swimming. They were all excited about the outing. Irene got all the children ready and waved good-bye to Evelyn as they headed for the bus.

The driver welcomed them with a smile. "You sure have nice children," he said. Irene smiled back, not sure how to answer him.

They rode to the pool and had a wonderful time splashing and playing in the refreshing water. Irene watched them all carefully, but she too enjoyed the day. It was such a relief to have fun with the children.

But soon it was time to return home. Irene gathered the children together, but Mike argued with her.

"I don't want to go home yet, Irene. I'm not going to ride on the bus, I'm going to walk home," he said.

At 12 years old, he towered over his 14-year-old sister. Irene thought for a moment, remembering that he had walked the distance before, then agreed that he could stay. He was really too old for her to argue with anyway. So she returned home on the bus with Laura, Willy, and Sammy.

Two hours later Irene stood in the kitchen preparing dinner and the phone rang. Evelyn answered. All that Irene heard was her mother scream, "What???" into the phone before she fainted.

Irene ran and picked up the receiver.

"What is it?" she asked anxiously, fearing for the life of her brother. The officer on the phone explained that Mike had been arrested for the sexual assault of two younger boys as they played around the pool. The blood drained from Irene's face.

"Just a minute, please," she said into the phone. She yelled for her dad to come quickly.

William took the phone and listened for a long time. He sank slowly into a chair and hid his face as the police explained the situation in greater detail. Then he hung up the phone and went to help Evelyn.

In the days to come various officials entered the house to question the family about Mike. Had they seen evidence of this behavior before? Did they know where he learned about these practices?

"Usually, this behavior is the result of the child having been molested himself by an older individual, sometimes a distant family member — a cousin or uncle. Is there any possibility of this?" one of the officials asked, making some attempt to understand the situation.

"Absolutely not. We've never heard of such a thing," Evelyn declared strongly.

"But, Mom, what about Gra . . .," Irene interjected, but was cut off immediately.

"You don't know what you're talking about. Go to the kitchen,

Irene," she said.

As the man turned to look at Irene, Evelyn glared at her, daring her to open her mouth again.

After the man left, Irene faced her mother about her question. "Why don't people just tell the truth, Mom? Why did you lie to that man and let him think that this is all Mike's fault? Why not tell them about Grandpa Jess?"

Evelyn looked with tired old eyes at her daughter.

"Because the truth hurts way too much, Irene."

In the days to follow, 12-year-old Mike was committed to a mental institution, in a ward filled with old men incarcerated for every imaginable offense. Evelyn had a complete nervous breakdown. She stayed in bed, unable to eat or go to the bathroom. She was unresponsive to the people around her. She did not even drink. After several days, William carried her gently in his arms to the car and took her to the hospital, wondering what to do.

The following week, Irene answered a knock at the door. Standing in the opening was a face straight out of Hades. She was six feet tall with long black hair and black eyes. She had pointed features and black painted fingernails that were more than an inch long. She looked like a fairy tale witch, or Elvira on television.

"Hello, my name is Nina. I'm the help your dad sent for."

And, thus, a new era dawned in the haunted house.

Nina had the strong, solid build of an athlete — left over remnants of her earlier years as a mud wrestler in Las Vegas. She had a strong personality and introduced the children to a variety of new fascinations. She brought with her a Ouija board, tarot cards, and other occult paraphernalia. And during Evelyn's absence, she taught the children many "tricks" with her toys.

Nina had a bizarre sense of entertainment. It gave her intense pleasure to frighten the children. She would allow them to play outside until dusk darkened the evening sky, then call them to come inside, hiding herself among the lilac bushes and jumping out like a screaming banshee to terrify them. Then she would roll in the grass, overcome with laughter at their fright.

Some nights, long after bedtime, she would dress in her usual all-black attire and drape herself with heavy tire chains. Then she would clank up the staircase like a vision from a Charles Dickens novel and burst into the children's room while they were sleeping, rattling her "shackles" and howling like a dog.

William was at the end of his rope — his son had been taken away and his wife was in the hospital nearly out of her mind, in addition to the normal monetary difficulties. When he returned home, the children tried to tell him about Nina. She would sit demurely in his presence, the very picture of respectability. The accusations against her angered him. He was up against the wall, having done all he could do, and did not want to hear anything bad about Nina. In his opinion, she had offered to help care for the children just when he needed her most.

He ignored their protestations, and when they pushed the issue, he beat them as he had seen Evelyn do so many times.

When Evelyn returned from the hospital, she and Nina took on that familiar stance of prize fighters maneuvering around each other before the first blows are struck. At first they fought, arguing vehemently with each other about the "care" of the children (which neither of them did), the cooking (their only trips to the kitchen were to get booze or give a chore to Irene or the children), and William. But eventually Evelyn capitulated, leaving Nina with the house and drowning her sorrows all day long at the Desmona Tavern.

The demonic influence in the household grew more powerful. Irene began seeing apparitions more often. One night she woke to see a huge hovering shadow enveloping her bed, like a gargantuan demon leering over her. Her breath caught in her throat and then she screamed out, "I plead the blood of Jesus over this house! In Jesus' name get out of here!" The presence left, then she shivered back under the sheet.

In Nina's presence Evelyn grew increasingly bitter toward William, and she soon filed for divorce. William was perplexed, not understanding why she wanted to split up with him. He felt that since they had been through so much together, why give it up now? But Evelyn was beyond reason.

They went to court, and in a surprising decision, William was awarded custody of all the children except Irene, who was not his legal daughter. He took the children and moved to Parkdale to be with their grandparents for the summer, hoping to find housing for the following school year. Nina returned to Alaska.

Now Irene was alone with Evelyn in the old creepy house.

Evelyn had continuous parties, still trying to run from the loneliness that haunted her. When Irene came home from school, she was expected to clean the house after every loud, drunken group. She deeply resented this expectation.

She often escaped to Shirley's house, going over to care for her baby nephew, David. Since her sister moved out, they had grown closer. They sat and talked, and Shirley would encourage her to stay in school and to stick with her music. Irene loved this companionship and missed her brothers and sisters terribly.

By August, Irene had enough of the drunken brawling life which now existed in the house on a daily basis. She was tired of her mother's excesses and cleaning up after drunks who trashed their house.

She called William in Parkdale and told him that if she couldn't come and live with him and her family, she would run away and never be heard from again. William quickly agreed, and came after Irene.

As she drove away with her stepfather, she whispered a prayer: "Thank you, Jesus, for getting me out of that spooky old house."

BLUE RIDGE

The Lord spoke with you face to face in the mount out of the midst of the fire.

Deuteronomy 5:4 AMP

And you said, Behold, the Lord our God has shown us His glory and His greatness, and we have heard His voice out of the midst of the fire; we have this day seen that God speaks with man and man still lives.

Deuteronomy 5:24 AMP

The street going up to Blue Ridge, outside Astoria, meandered through thick forest and up to the crest of a hill covered with small duplexes. They angled in odd directions and looked like wildly colored mobile homes glued haphazardly to the side of the steep hill. Some were blue, some yellow, painted whatever was handy to help cover the cheap construction of abandoned military housing.

Children wandered about everywhere, unsupervised, playing stickball or hopscotch in the street. Weeds grew high, and trash blew unnoticed, gluing itself to trees or the sides of houses. Most houses displayed a collection of cars on wood planks or concrete blocks waiting in vain for mechanical attention.

The family's new home was the right side of a peeling blue and white duplex, built into the side of the hill.

That summer they moved in — Ruth, Laura, Willy, Sammy, Irene, and their father William. The children were soon settled in school. Irene was in high school, and the other kids were in various grades, with Ruth in Head Start. William got back to his fishing and left the children in Irene's capable hands. At times, he was gone for days, returning with fresh fish and money. Irene would buy the groceries, plan the meals, cook, clean, help with homework, and make sure the children had clean clothes for school. She would comb their hair and hug them, and try to tell them every day that she loved them. Everything seemed peaceful and right for the first time since they had moved to Astoria when Irene was a child. But, as usual, the peace was short lived.

In October, William prepared to take his boat from Astoria to Cascade Locks to make annual repairs and fish for salmon. He called Irene in to sit at the table and he told her that certain arrangements had been made for his absence.

"I've called Nina to come and watch you kids while I'm gone," he said.

Irene's face went sheet white, "No, Dad, please not Nina again."

"What's wrong, girl?" William asked.

"I can do it. I've done good so far. I get your dinner on time and the kids are doing okay. Please Dad. Did I do something wrong? Let me fix it."

"No, girl. Ruthie has to get picked up from Head Start and you can't drive. Besides you need to have an adult with you. I'm going to be gone too long to leave you alone."

Irene could see he had his mind set. She tried again.

"But, Dad, she is bad around the kids. She tries to scare them, and she threatens them with knives and jumps out of the bushes and stuff." In her frustration the words poured out. "They don't feel safe with her. She's really scary!"

She backed away at the annoyance in his face. He did not believe her.

"That's enough. I don't want to hear your stories. Nina is nice enough to come and help. There's nobody else I can ask to come."

"But, Dad, she scares me. She drinks too much."

His face got stony with anger.

"This is not your decision to make. She is coming."

A few days later, the children scrambled off the school bus down the street, their merry, happy songs riding the aimless wanderings of the wind. A can was kicked, a joke told, and Puddles wound his way through their skipping legs barking joyfully. Irene opened the door and they piled inside, coming to an abrupt and startled halt. Nina was home.

She sat at the table chopping up salad with a large carving knife. She turned from the salad and picked up her drink from the table, the carving knife still in the other hand. A long cigarette drooped from her mouth, and her steel gray eyes stared like a black widow eyeing a struggling fly.

Nina was, if anything, worse than before. Now without the presence of Evelyn, and in William's extensive absences, she was free to play her vicious games with the minds of the children. If a child didn't do what she said or did not have the right look on their face when she wanted them to smile or respond to her in some way, she took the breadboard, a 12-inch square piece of wood with a handle, and smacked them against the side of the head. And if they cried, the punishment was even worse.

Irene, as the oldest, tried to step into these situations, pleading, "Please don't hit them with that breadboard!"

"If you don't shut up, I'll take this carving knife and cut your throat. I've killed people before, don't you know that?" she leered menacingly, and Irene believed her threat completely.

And so they lived in the tension of potential violence vacillating with times of faked kindness. If a child did not hold his fork right or forgot some rule at the table, he could be appropriately reprimanded, as would happen in a normal family, or he could have his food dumped on the floor and be forced to eat it.

"You're acting like a dog, so you can eat like one," Nina would say.

Nina took special delight in taunting Sammy. He had platinum white hair and a chunky little body. He was quiet child, not often taking part in the conversation, but when he had a word, it was a kind word for other people. He felt Nina's negative attention all the time. He grew afraid to bring his papers home from school, avoiding her wrathful insults and eventual punishment.

One morning, Sammy searched the house looking for his one and only pair of shoes. He was frantic, hunting for them to wear to school. The other children helped him look. Sammy remembered taking the shoes off the previous afternoon to go play, saving them for school, but they were not where he left them.

Nina raged at Sammy to find the shoes. She stalked around the house with the belt, randomly smacking any child that got too close.

"Find those shoes, or you'll get a spanking and stay in your room the whole day. No television, no food, no nothing." She was angry, but seemed to be enjoying the situation.

"Please, no. I'll find them." But the shoes were not to be found. The other children left and went to school without him.

That afternoon when the children got off the bus, there stood Sammy.

"Hey, Sammy! Did you find your shoes?"

"Yeah," he said, looking down and scuffing his toes in the dust.

"She hid them in the basement. I didn't even go down to that basement yesterday. I know it was Nina."

"Oh, yeah. Sure," said Irene. She was used to people not believing her "stories," so she didn't believe Sammy.

Sammy looked up at Irene, big tears welling up in his bright blue eyes.

"I'm telling the truth." And he walked off.

This incident, and similar ones, were a regular occurrence with Nina running the household. Some days when Nina would be very drunk, she would pull the children's ears until they yelped, or squeeze their fingers with her strong hands, picking them up off the floor. Many afternoons the children sat like little statues lined up on the couch, thinking that any action might set her off.

Each trip home from school brought new anxieties. Most days the children waited for one another so they could enter the house as a group; there is strength in numbers. But Nina caught on to this ploy and sometimes would meet the children at the bus.

Once in a while Nina would be sober and coherent. At times, she would even cook or clean. But for the most part she was a terrifying presence waiting for some new vicious game to play.

Nina hated for Irene to play the flute or sing. When she was gone to the store or running an errand, Irene would sneak out her flute and practice. If she lost track of the time and was still playing when Nina returned, Nina would grab the flute case and chase Irene through the house, beating her with it.

But music remained Irene's first love. She sang with the Madrigal group, and her beautiful voice was in great demand for weddings and other local events. Irene reveled in the attention, thinking that even though she couldn't do anything else right, she could sing like an angel. Music was slowly becoming her god.

Irene grew to fear Nina with her whole being. Nina's abuse of authority made Irene suspicious and resentful of all authority, including the Lord's. She did not trust anyone. She saw other people as having a facade. She resented her mother for forcing her to care for her in her drunken stupors. She resented the kids for needing her as a mother, and costing her a childhood. She resented William for never believing her, never trusting her judgment. She resented the authorities for taking her away from her beloved grandmother, and her grandmother for not fighting for her freedom. She resented her past teachers for their cruelty and lack of understanding. And she deeply resented Grandpa Jess.

As time passed, she developed a new philosophy: The only one she could trust was herself. She tried, at times, to read the Bible, but she could not comprehend the words. It was a totally closed book to her, and this made God seem even farther away. The times when she had felt the Lord's presence in the past, even His voice speaking directly to her, drifted farther and farther into her memory as the malignant presence of Nina overwhelmed her thinking.

Two weeks before Halloween, Irene got off the bus and walked up her street. As she neared the house, she saw the old green couch outside in the weeds of the front "lawn." She ran quickly to the door to find out what was happening. Nina looked at Irene from her post at the kitchen table.

"Why did you pull the couch outside?" Irene asked, wondering if Nina had totally lost her mind.

"Oh, it caught on fire, so I had to haul the old thing outside."

"Well, how did it catch on fire?" Irene insisted. She looked at Nina expectantly.

"There was a cigarette caught between the two cushions. That's how it caught on fire." Irene looked at her in disgust. It was their only piece of furniture, a saggy old couch, but it was better than the floor.

"Well, let's see if I can fix it up." She went outside and checked to make sure the fire no longer smoldered in the deep cushions. Then she and the children struggled to get it back inside and covered the damage with a blanket.

When William came home, he questioned Irene about the couch, but it was obvious that Nina had already set her story in motion. William accused Irene of smoking and burning up the couch. Irene told him that she did not smoke, and that the couch was burned up while she was still at school. He did not believe her again.

One week later, William left for a trip to visit his parents in Parkdale. That Thursday, Nina picked the younger kids up from school, while Irene stayed later for Madrigal practice. She returned home to find all the kids sitting on the floor crying and Nina laughing her loud drunken laugh from the kitchen.

"What's going on?" she asked, eyeing Nina cautiously.

"Oh, we're just having fun," she slurred. Irene wondered, "At whose expense?"

She picked up Ruthie and comforted her, still keeping a wary eye on Nina.

"Come and try this, Irene." Nina turned from the kitchen cutting board with the knife in one hand and a two-inch-long green pepper in her other hand, the hottest Mexican variety.

"I don't want to eat that," said Irene, still eyeing the butcher knife.

"Come on, you better eat it, or I'll force you to eat it!" she stumbled with the knife toward Irene, laughing her high-pitched, witchy laugh.

"Don't get mad, Nina. I'll eat your pepper." Irene took the green pepper from Nina's hand and gingerly bit into it. Pepper juice splattered in her mouth, burning every surface. She choked with the shock at the unbelievably hot taste. Even her lips scalded at the touch of the pungent liquid.

"Water, water!" Tears streamed down her face.

"Not yet sweetie. Eat it all! You have to eat the whole thing. If you don't eat it, I'll make the kids eat it." She laughed with glee and swung the knife in the air nearly losing her drunken balance.

She regained her stance and stared diabolically at Irene. The kids, one by one edged out of the room and ran to their bedrooms to hide.

Their eyes met and time stood still for a moment, then Irene put the whole pepper in her mouth, quickly choking it down, and ran to the bathroom for water — anything, to kill the searing taste. Nina bent over and then fell on the floor, rolling in uncontrollable laughter. Irene drank some water and did the best she could to remove the scorching taste. She stared at herself in the mirror and wondered what would be next.

"Irene, come here." She cringed and steeled herself to return to the kitchen.

"I'm making us some drinks," Nina said, "then we're all going for a nice long ride." Irene's heart leaped with hope. Nina might behave and calm down if she was around other people.

"Okay, Nina, that's a good idea," Irene replied.

They gathered the children together and headed for the car. As they bustled the kids into the back seat of the old wing-tipped sedan, Nina turned to Irene.

"Here, take the keys. It's time you learned to drive."

"Nina, I can't drive. I'm only 15. I have never driven before, and I don't know how." Irene was getting very nervous.

"I'm too drunk to drive. Get behind that wheel, you stupid idiot!" There was no backing out of it. Irene got behind the wheel and started the car. She gingerly edged the vehicle down the steep road and drove slowly towards town. Nina mixed a drink for Irene and handed it to her as they drove. Irene looked at the drink, hiding her deep disgust and searched her mind for an idea to end the nightmare.

Then Nina said "Let's go to Shirley's house. We haven't seen your sister in a while."

"Yeah, that's a good idea."

They stopped in front of Shirley's old Victorian house and went inside. Shirley sat on her couch with the baby, Donny, while David, the three year old played on the rug. They sat and talked for a while, then Shirley said she needed a break from David.

Nina said, "Oh, let him come with us, Irene can take care of him."

Irene looked at Shirley, hoping she could see how drunk Nina was and the potential danger of the situation. But Shirley was lost in her own plans, thinking only of the possibility that she could have a night off.

"Sure, Shirley," said Nina. "Find a sitter for the baby and go have yourself a good time. We'll take David." Irene went into the kitchen for a glass of water, thinking frantically of how to avoid adding another child to the situation.

"Shirley, could you come here?" She called her sister to the kitchen. Shirley came in and Irene drew her aside.

"Nina's drunk, she's really bad drunk. I need some help, I'm afraid of her." Shirley looked at Irene with disgust.

"Oh, Nina's just fine. Quit telling your stories and go get in the car." Irene realized the futility of arguing. She went out with the children and David and they left.

"You still have to drive, you know." Nina was enjoying Irene's discomfort.

"Why don't we just go home? I'll make some dinner and you can go take a nap. Let's do that. That sounds like fun. I don't really want to do anything or go anywhere." She tried to beg Nina to go home.

"Nope, we're going to Seaside."

Irene gasped. The town was 20 miles away on the coastal highway. She felt her heart drop to her feet. How could she possibly drive that far?

As they started through town, Nina wanted to stop at a tavern for more liquor. She came back out, accompanied by a tall older man who smelled of booze and body odor.

"Nina, we can't take him. There's no room."

"Yes, there is. Get in." Nina glared at Irene, angry that she had been questioned.

They headed for Seaside, the car quiet with tension except for the two drunks in the front seat, laughing and touching each other with obvious sexual intent. Irene drove slowly and carefully and eventually the long ride ended. She drove them through the streets of Seaside as the nature of the couple's conversation changed from the bawdy exchanges to half-hearted bickering and later to an open argument. The man started to threaten Nina, hitting her and pulling her hair.

"Get out of this car!" Nina was starting to get angry.

"I ain't getting out of this car!" He grabbed at her breast, and she turned toward him in the car, kicking and hitting at him.

"Stop the car, Irene."

"What?"

"I said, stop the car now, Irene!" She slowed the car, watching for traffic in the middle of the street. Nina reached past the man and grabbed the door handle, opening it faster than the man could react. Then she drew her long legs up and kicked him forcefully out of the still moving car. She grabbed the door and slammed it shut.

"Move it, Irene. We're getting out of here, fast." She swung her legs around and put her high-heeled foot on top of Irene's, crushing her foot onto the accelerator.

"I said, 'Go!'"

Irene struggled to control the car until the foot was removed, choking on the powerful fear that gripped her. When or how would this nightmare end?

The return home was relatively uneventful as Irene learned to control the car with the periodic intervention of Nina's foot on the accelerator. She heaved a huge sigh of relief, thinking the worst was over. Surely now everything would settle down.

They went inside and Irene fixed some dinner and got the children in pajamas. She watched Nina mix drink after drink, and hoped that she would pass out or go to bed. But then, as the kids started for their bedrooms, Nina grabbed David, the three year old, and started wrestling with him on the floor. She poked him in the stomach and then got up and swung him around in the air by one foot. He cried and struggled to escape her hold, but he could not get away.

"Nina, you don't need to do that stuff," Irene tried to intervene.

Nina turned on Irene and started grabbing her earrings, trying to pull them out through the skin.

"I'll play with him if I want to. He likes it. Don't you see that, you stupid girl. You go to bed." The other children huddled in the corner, in utter terror. Irene hesitated only a moment. When Nina turned again towards her, she made her escape to the bedroom.

Once in her room, Irene racked her brain, searching for what to do. She listened to the cries of the children in the living room, looking around for a weapon or a way to get help. She caught sight of the window and remembered that Willy had shown her only days ago how to jump out and roll with the landing to avoid injury. Willy had even practiced on the two-story side of the house. She ran for the window, jumped out and raced to the neighbor's house. She banged on the door and a lady answered.

"Please help me. Let me use your phone. I've got to get my sister to come and help us."

The woman hesitated, then let Irene in to call Shirley. She answered the phone in a sleepy, bored voice. Irene begged her to come and get the children, telling her that Nina had lost control. She told her what was happening to David and that it had to be stopped. She sighed with relief as Shirley promised to come.

Irene waited at the neighbor's house until Shirley arrived with a male friend, looking irritated with the interruption. The door to the house was open and the sound of children crying could clearly be heard outside. Nina came outside and talked to Shirley and the man for several minutes, laughing and joking as though there was nothing wrong.

Irene walked towards them, close enough to hear the conversation.

"Oh, it's just Irene again. She was telling the kids scary stories and got them all upset. But they're okay now. I just can't let her do that again. She's been drinking and she's rolling on the floor and playing too rough with them." They all turned and looked as Irene walked toward them.

"Why do you always cause trouble, Irene? Nina is just fine, there's nothing wrong with her." Shirley had immediately believed Nina's story. "If you don't stop this crap we're going to send you back to Mom. If you don't go back in there and go to bed we're going to tie you to the bed and make you stay."

Shirley and the man got into the car and drove away. Irene stood and watched them leave, hope dying as their taillights faded in the distance.

"If you don't go to bed and shut up about this, I'm going to beat you." Nina glared at Irene, then they both went inside.

Irene went to bed, but Nina kept the little kids up. Unhappy noises drifted down the hallway and into Irene's bedroom. She had to make another attempt. Again she jumped out the high window, rolling to the ground and headed to the neighbor's house. This time the lady was more hesitant about helping.

"I need to call the police," said Irene.

"Look honey, we want to help, but we know about Nina and the knives. We don't want any trouble."

"But I need some help now!" Irene's eyes filled with tears, afraid of what could be happening to the children. The woman's face changed from a look of fearful hesitation to a look of terror as she saw Nina coming towards them, the butcher knife held prominently in her hand.

"You get home, or I'm going to kill you!" She yelled at Irene and then to the woman. "This is none of your business. You'd better keep out of it." She shouted profanities at the woman, who had now slammed and locked her door.

Irene went back to the house and took the children to their rooms, finally able to put them to bed. Nina followed these proceedings, knife in hand. Again, she threatened Irene.

"Nobody's going to believe one word you say," she said, gritting her teeth like a rabid dog. "Go to bed, or you'll die!"

Irene ran quickly to her bedroom and pulled the covers up high around her.

Several hours passed when Irene woke from her nervous sleep. She smelled the acrid stench of melting plastic, and a new fear dawned in her head. She jumped out of bed and ran into the hall. Sammy ambled half asleep, towards the bathroom.

"Sammy, are you okay?" She asked softly.

"Yep," he said.

She watched him disappear into the bathroom, then yelled to Nina from her door.

"Nina, is everything okay? I smell smoke. Is the couch on fire again?" Gray smoke drifted down the hall.

Nina came to the hallway and answered.

"I have everything under control. Get in your bed, or I'm coming in there after you."

"But we need to get the kids out. There's so much smoke."

"They'll be fine. Get back to bed. Now!"

Irene obeyed, wondering what was going on, yet not daring to push the matter further. Eventually she returned to a fitful sleep, thinking maybe Nina was cooking something and had burned it on the stove. It was about 2 a.m.

At about 4 a.m., Irene felt someone shaking her awake, but when she opened her eyes, no one was there. She heard loud and unmistakable sounds of fire crackling, loud sounds, high pitched, like glass breaking. She quickly grabbed her sisters, Laura and Ruth, and threw open the window. She hurled Laura out the window, and heard her cry as she hit the ground.

"Why are you throwing me out the window?" Laura cried to Irene.

"There's a fire! Run! Run!" Irene threw Ruth out toward Laura.

Then Nina flung open the bedroom door. Through the opening, Irene saw flames licking the far wall of the hallway. Nina had covered herself with an old wool blanket, her long stringy hair hanging out in disarray.

"The house is on fire!"

"I know! Let's get the kids out," Irene said. Nina stared at her, blankly. "I'll go get the fire department. I got Ruth and Laura out, you go get the boys."

Nina did not move. Irene screamed at her, "Go get the boys!"

"I will! I will!" Nina turned and fled out of the bedroom.

Irene jumped out the window, screaming, "Help us! Help us! Please, help us!" Her voice rose louder and louder, "Isn't anybody listening? Please help us!"

She reached the neighbor's house and once again pounded on the door. The woman peeked out through the curtain.

"There's a fire. Please, I've got to use your phone!" Her panic finally got through to the woman and the door opened. Irene ran for the phone and grabbed the telephone book. She located the number and dialed the Tongue Point Fire Department, located just over the hill.

"Come to Blue Ridge. There's a fire! I need you to come. Right now!"

"I'm sorry. That is out of our jurisdiction. You'll have to call the Astoria Fire Department."

"What's the number? Please help me!"

"You'll have to look it up." Irene banged down the phone and grabbed the book again. She located the next fire department and quickly dialed. She frantically told them about the fire.

"We don't send trucks to Blue Ridge unless life is endangered.

Is everybody out of the house?"

"Yes, everybody's out."

"Then call Tongue Point. They can take care of the fire."

"I did, I did. They said to call you." Her agitation grew as she struggled with their questions. "Why are you asking me all these questions. The house will burn down if you don't come."

Over the shoulder of her neighbor Irene saw Nina come into the room.

"Nina, did you get the boys out?" Nina stared. "Nina, did you get the boys out?" she demanded. A cold dread crept over her heart as she looked into Nina's face.

"Well, where are they?" Irene screamed.

"Willy's jumped out, but the other boys are still in the house."

"You've got to be kidding," she was shrieking now.

Irene turned back to the phone, "There are kids in there. There are kids in there! You gotta come — now!" She threw the phone down and headed out the door.

People began gathering in clusters in the early morning darkness. Irene tried to go in the front door of the flaming house, scorching her hands and hair on the burning door post, but hands caught her, and someone said, "You can't go in there."

"Yes, I can. Let me go. Let me go." She broke free and ran across the street. Someone took the old green and white car out of gear and pushed it a safe distance from the flames.

"Anybody got a ladder? The boys are still in there. Anybody? Boost me up! Come on!" Several people ran with Irene down the steep bank to the back of the house. As they rounded the edge of the building a fireball exploded a red and orange blaze out the window of the boy's bedroom. The house was gone in minutes.

Irene fell on the ground and lay there, her body racked with hysterical sobbing. Someone picked her up and carried her to a waiting car. Ruth, Laura and Willy were already in the car. They were all taken to the hospital. Irene was still raging at the unbelievable fact that the boys were still in the house. She clawed at the rear window watching the house in the distance. As they headed down the steep hill, the fire truck passed the car.

"Willy, how did you get out?" He was crying and holding his ears, already swelling in large painful blisters. "What happened?"

"I don't know, Reenie. I woke up," he spoke through thick

sobs, "I woke up and the whole wall was on fire and I just jumped out. I never thought about getting them, Irene. I'm sorry."

"What about Puddles? Where's my dog?"

"I don't know, Irene. The last I saw he was lying on the floor next to Sammy. I just don't know." He turned his face away, big tears washing down on the burned places. He was burned all over his ears, his hands, and upper arms, but the real pain was the loss of his brother and cousin.

William was called in Parkdale and immediately returned to seek out Nina for an explanation. Then he talked to Irene and told her that Puddles was found on the floor right next to Sammy. He began to question her about the fire. She could tell immediately that something was amiss. She told him how the whole day had gone from bad to worse and how she had jumped out the window to try and get help. She told him about Nina's drunken games and how scared the kids had been. She told him about calling Shirley and the police. He just looked at her. Then he shook his head. Nina had already told him that Irene was smoking and had started the fire. Irene hung her head. Now, she thought, there was no way that he would believe her.

God Granted Us An Angel

Light-haired, bright-eyed baby boy,
You were only here nine years.
But you brought sunshine
To everyone who was close to you.
If Willy did something wrong
You always took the blame
You couldn't see anybody else get hurt.

Sammy, oh baby boy, you were so good
You thought no one cared, I cared
But you went on day after day,
Smiling and laughing.
Nine years is much too short a time,
For someone like you.
The night you died,
A part of me died too.
Sammy, if you can hear me . . .
I miss you.

Irene Taylor

FRANKLIN STREET

Listen! My lover! Look! Here he comes, leaping across the mountains, bounding over the hills. My lover is like a gazelle or a young stag. Look! There he stands behind our wall, gazing through the windows, peering through the lattice. My lover spoke and said to me, "Arise, my darling, my beautiful one, and come with me. See! The winter is past; the rains are over and gone. Flowers appear on the earth; the season of singing has come, the cooing of doves is heard in our land. The fig tree forms its early fruit; the blossoming vines spread their fragrance. Arise, come, my darling; my beautiful one, come with me."

Song of Solomon 2:8-13 NIV

On a rainy day, several days later, Sammy and David were buried next to each other in two small white caskets. No one comforted Irene — no hug, no word of encouragement. No one showed any indication that they did not believe the whole incident was her fault. She suffered alone and in silence.

The children stayed with William's friends while he looked for a new house. Nina stayed in the hospital for several days having treatment for emotional distress and a few minor burns.

Sleep came hard for Irene. In her restless dreams she heard the roar and the crackle of fire crawling through the house. It haunted her. Then, one night, she sat on the floor, almost afraid to go to bed and dream her awful dreams. She sat alone, despairing of all that had happened.

Suddenly the room opened up and became very bright. She looked around, wondering if she was dreaming, but realized that she was totally awake. The Lord Jesus appeared in front of her, as real as the floor on which she sat. She looked at Him, but she could not clearly see His face. He wore a glistening white robe — brighter than any earthly fabric.

Then they were no longer in the room and she stood by His side going up a small hill. Sammy and David were there, holding hands, wearing the same pajamas that she had dressed them in the night of the fire. She recognized David's pajamas with the little panel in back. He always wanted only one flap snapped so he could go to the bathroom by himself in the night, so the other snap hung down across his hip. Sammy was hanging on to Jesus, and David held Sammy's other hand.

The Lord spoke to Irene in a voice so gentle and tender with understanding that her broken heart melted: "Who can be a better father for these two boys than I?"

She looked at Him.

"When you come home to be with Me, you will be with them also, Irene." He smiled at her. Tears streamed down her face as the hurt dissolved in His gentle presence. They all stood together, then turned and walked up the hill. Irene could see the grass and how vividly green it was, different from earth, clean and healthy and growing. She could feel the peaceful wind blowing against her hair. Tree leaves rustled in the breeze. They glistened and shone with an iridescence totally different from earthly trees. In the distance a small stream gurgled between the trees, the water shimmering with rainbow colors.

When they reached the crest of the hill, Jesus paused.

"You have to stop right here, at the top of this hill. I cannot let you go past this point, because then you will want to be with them, but I'll let you see this far. Know that it's okay and I have them with me. You don't have to be their mom anymore. I'll be their dad and I'll take care of them."

She looked at Him, wanting with all her soul to follow them down the hill. He smiled at her and then they walked away. Then she saw Puddles scampering rapidly after them to catch up. They faded in the distance, and Irene found herself back on the floor in the house of William's friends.

Soon William found a place and the kids moved in. People in the community responded to their terrible loss in the fire, taking the children downtown for new shoes and clothing. The children had better garments after the disaster than they had before.

One afternoon, a journalist came to the house and wanted to clarify some details about the fire, as the lack of response from the fire departments had caused a local furor, particularly because of the death of the two boys. William would not let the man speak with Irene. He said, "All she does is tell stories. If you want the truth, I'll tell you what happened." Irene was again crushed by this implication of her "guilt."

After a time, William left on another fishing trip and asked Nina to return to "care" for the remaining children. Immediately after he left, things returned to the way they had before. They had a new breadboard, which she broke in over the heads of the kids. She had a shiny new knife to brandish in their frightened faces. Nothing had changed.

Irene borrowed a flute from school to continue her music and she determined to carry on in the face of her still broken heart. The vision from heaven warmed her in her private moments, but its brightness would fade in the face of Nina's continued presence.

One afternoon, in the cold of November, the kids had come home from school and were outside playing with the neighbor kids. Nina came outside, absolutely plastered with the effects of alcohol. She could barely walk she was so drunk.

"Come on kids. Let's go for a ride." She looked at them, daring someone to challenge her. The children piled into the car, neighbor kids and all. A couple of the older children took off running, leaving the younger ones with no choice but to comply. Irene was grateful that she was not forced to drive again.

This time they headed up to the mountains on a long winding road. The sky darkened with clouds and rain pummeled the roof of the old car. Farther and farther they went, past the end of the pavement, up the old logging road. The ruts grew deeper and the streaming water thickened the mud into deep puddles. Irene yelped with surprise as a small animal appeared directly in the path of the coming car.

"You're going to hit that animal, Nina."

Nina stomped on the accelerator, aiming directly for the spiny porcupine. They ran right over the animal and she swerved to a stop. Nina opened the door and stumbled into the pouring rain. Suddenly, the back door opened, and she shook the bleeding porcupine in the children's faces, then threw it into the trunk. They screamed.

"Shut up. That's dinner," she said. Their eyes got as big as saucers as they thought about eating road kill.

She clambered back into the driver's seat and the car groaned with effort, trying to escape the muddy pothole. Again she exited the car and then saw the punctured tire rapidly losing all its air.

She cursed vehemently and threw the back door open.

"Everybody out. Come on. Don't waste my time!" The children crawled out into the pouring rain. She took them over to a pile of cut branches and dug into them to find dry wood. Soon she had a small fire started and the children huddled close to keep warm. All the children were crying with fear and cold.

She picked up a stick and waved it at the kids, "Quit that crying, or I'll make it worse." They quieted down immediately.

She settled herself on a rock near the fire and said, "We have to build this fire so the wild animals won't come and eat you." The children peered around in even more fright. "Now I'm going to tell you some stories, and they are true stories, so don't interrupt."

In the morning, Nina walked down the muddy road to get help. She left the children alone in the woods for hours. They were finally rescued when she returned with a man in an old green pickup truck who took them all home. The neighbors and the police were there waiting.

The parents of the young children assaulted the truck, screaming and yelling at Nina when they drove up. The police drew her aside and demanded an explanation for the children's absence.

Nina just said, "They're not hurt. They had fun. What's the big deal?"

After talking her way out of the mess, she got a neighbor to drive her up and pull the car out of the mud and fix the tire. When she returned, she told Irene to get the kids together. Then she went to the trunk of the car and got the porcupine, left without benefit of refrigeration all night long. The children sat in sickening silence as she skinned the road kill and chopped up the pieces with a huge kitchen cleaver.

"See, this is going to be great," she said. "You'll be the only kids you know who ever ate porcupine." She cooked the animal and forced the children to eat the stringy, bitter meat.

When William returned home, he was met by a group of neighbors who told him in no uncertain terms what had happened. Plus, in the kitchen, he saw the remnants of the porcupine dinner. Finally he could no longer deny the truth about who and what Nina was. It was a hard truth. He cared about Nina, and she had filled a certain void after his divorce from Evelyn. But he finally accepted what everyone else had known all along — that Nina was a vicious, cruel, unreliable alcoholic, certainly incapable of caring for his children. There was a huge fight, and the next day Irene came home from school to find Nina gone for good.

Irene returned to her accustomed duties, caring for the children, and trying to deal with the gnawing sense of despair and loss after the fire. She was sad and lonely.

Shirley had introduced her to several of the boys she had dated before her marriage. And one afternoon, when visiting Shirley, she ran into a school acquaintance. He invited her for coffee and she went, enjoying the company. They spent the afternoon together and had dinner. Later he took her home.

William was gone on one of his overnight fishing trips when they returned to the house. The children met Irene at the door and asked if they could spend the night at the neighbor's. She said fine and turned to say good night to the boy, but he refused to leave. The children sped by them out the door.

"Look," she said. "You can't come in. My dad's not home, and I'll get in real trouble."

He smiled at her, his attractive blue eyes dancing with amusement, and said, "Oh, I just want to come in and visit for a while."

She looked at him, wanting not to offend, but wishing he would leave.

"Okay. You can come in for just a minute. Then you have to go," she said.

"Fine," he said, entering the empty house.

He made himself comfortable on the couch. Irene made them

some coffee and they talked for a while. Then Irene told him that he had to leave. He leaned over and grabbed her arm, forcing her down on the couch. She screamed and struggled away from him. Then, as she attempted to fight him off, he took from her the one vestige of innocence she had left from all those times with Grandpa Jess, the virginity she had promised God she would save for marriage. In silence, he left.

After the rape, she cried bitter tears for hours, angry beyond imagination at the boy who violated her and furious beyond belief at her God who had allowed it. If God cared, why had this happened, piled on top of all the other repulsive incidents of her life? It was the last straw.

William searched several weeks for a reliable and safe person to stay with the children. He asked his Aunt Eunice, his mother's sister, if she could come and care for his family. She agreed, and soon joined the family in their new home.

Aunt Eunice was a retired school teacher. Her presence added many new facets to the lives of William's children. She was kind and loving, stern with her discipline, but never cruel or abusive. She enjoyed helping the kids with their homework. She was the most normal person that the children had around in a long time.

Aunt Eunice stayed with them for about two months, then left for a brief trip to Portland, planning to return with all her belongings and permanently care for the children. As she drove back to Portland, a truck sideswiped her van, and she was killed instantly. Once again the care of the children fell into Irene's hands.

Irene slowly recovered her senses after the deep emotional shock of the rape and losing her brother, nephew, and Aunt Eunice. She was different now in some vital ways. Gone was the little victim cowering in the corner waiting to be battered into submission.

On the day she grabbed the broomstick from her mother, some dormant strength began to bloom and grow in her personality. She called upon this strength now, no longer taking the abuse lying down. This new persona, twisted by her life experiences and unguided by any positive examples around her, was as warped in its own way as her old personality.

In this new mode, Irene envisioned herself as taking control of every situation in her life. She was no longer the slave labor in the kitchen. Instead, she saw herself as overseer of the household. No longer was she the poor little Cinderella with the voice of an angel, but the budding prima donna, difficult and demanding.

She saw herself as the god of her own life. And she would take care of herself. No longer did she see God as caring or even wanting to be concerned for her. She had no desire to hear His voice, or to know His thoughts about her actions. She was in a deep rebellion against Him. She turned on Him in her anger and blamed Him for every foul thing that had ever happened to her.

Her growing independence from God was supported by the increasing affluence of her family's living condition. At the same time that she turned her back on God, people in the community began to give great gifts to the family. In her twisted mind, Irene felt almost as if the farther she pushed away from God, the better things became.

After the fire they received a nice new dining room table with chairs. The kids had beautiful clothes, some brand new. Gimrey's Shoe Store in Astoria invited the whole family down to be fitted with new fashionable shoes and socks that fit. The children had never been in a shoe store before. It was wonderful!

These blessings were given to the family out of a heartfelt response by the community to help them out after losing their belongings in the fire. Many citizens were saddened and angered that the fire departments had not responded to the call.

A few months after the fire, during Irene's sophomore year in high school, she was so tired of not being allowed to participate in activities that she begged William to allow her to attend a dance at Clatsop Community College. She dressed carefully in her new black and white shirt with matching black pants and bravely walked onto the college grounds. The music blared out of the campus gym.

She went inside, looking for her high school friends, and she mingled with them for a while. Then she noticed a tall, handsome, slender man with black curly hair. He looked back at her with smiling interest and eventually asked her to dance. After three dances, he left.

Irene was crushed. She had enjoyed his company so much.

"Oh, well," she said, and continued on around the hall, talking and laughing with acquaintances.

Suddenly there was a hand on her elbow. "I can't find anybody better, so I'm going to dance with you the rest of the night."

"Don't I know you from somewhere?" he asked later.

"I met you when you were a senior and I was a freshman in the special concert. I was invited to play the flute with your school band." He smiled, remembering.

"That's right! I did meet you then," he said.

He bought her a soda and told her his name was Chris Taylor. From that moment on they were inseparable.

In the following months, their friendship developed into a kind of love. Her knight in shining armor would roar up in front of the house on his 350 Super Hawk motorcycle. William did not mind the motorcycle and liked Chris from the very beginning. His suspicious nature, however, led him to have Irene's boyfriend investigated. But after Chris passed this muster, he was accepted without reservation.

Chris and Irene went to movies and long walks up to the Astor Column. They would sit and talk for hours on the front porch watching ships sail in and out of the mouth of the Columbia River. The city lights glimmered in the distance as they sat having those deep and meaningful discussions of young love. Chris called her every single day, and they talked for hours about endless teenage subjects. They went to dances and dinners. They spent time with Chris' stepfather, mother, and younger brother at their home.

Chris accompanied Irene on her many singing engagements around the area. They attended the Methodist church together and had Sunday dinner with Chris' mom and dad.

Irene and her friend Anne had been invited to play with the Seaside Symphony Orchestra. Chris would take Irene to the concerts and listen to her play the flute, waiting patiently to take her home.

She would accompany Chris to basketball games where he played in the pep band. She was invited to join the college choir, where Chris already sang. They had wonderful times together.

Over the next two years their relationship deepened. Irene slowly faced the fact that Chris would graduate in the spring from junior college and in the fall would transfer to the university. She was broken-hearted at their separation, but realized that it was inevitable. Irene still had to complete her senior year in high school.

They parted tearfully, and Chris pressed a piece of paper, a poem, into Irene's hand. Then he headed down to Oregon State University in Corvallis, and she forced herself to concentrate on her school work.

My Darling Irene

Who kindles the lines of my chilled heart,
Who takest away all feelings of sadness,
Whose bright smile fills
My lonely soul with warmth,
And who will I always love
And be loved
Until her soul is mingling with mine
For all blessed eternity.
I love thee Irene

Chris

By now Irene was in full possession of her life's rudder. She carefully assessed her situation and decided in a cold and logical manner that she no longer needed to act as mother to the children. It was William's responsibility to provide for their care. She thought about what she wanted to do and approached Chris' parents, asking them for permission to move in and live with them for her senior year in high school.

They had previously thought about getting someone to come and live with them, to help with the housework and keep an eye on Scott, Chris' nine-year-old brother. They considered getting a college student, but Irene was someone they knew and liked.

Irene asked William for permission to live with them. At first he said "no," but she persisted, reminding him that she was 18 years old and could go just as well without his blessing.

"But Irene," he said, puzzled. "Who's going to take care of the kids? Who's going to pay your way?"

"Dad, I've taken care of those kids for my whole life, and you know it. Now it's somebody else's turn. I have taken a job at the hospital for after school, and all I have to pay for is my clothes anyway." She asked his permission, but it was clear that her mind was made up.

"It's not that I don't love you, Dad. I do love you. But I just can't do this any more. Please let me go."

In a few days, Chris' mother and step-father, Myrna and Bob, came to help Irene pack and to take her home with them. Irene loved living with Chris' family. Myrna and Bob were very kind and supportive of her efforts in music and school. She got along famously with Chris' little brother, playing basketball and kid games with him.

In the mornings, she got up to a clean house, sometimes cooking breakfast herself, and other times being served by Myrna or Bob. The family shared in the household chores and did not lean heavily on Irene.

After school three or four days a week, Irene worked as an aide in the hospital for two to five hours. Some evenings she came straight home from work; other days she went to perform at a wedding, funeral, or other community event. She participated in plays and musicals in school.

Most of the time either Bob or Myrna or both attended these events, sitting near the front where Irene could see them clearly. As she stood at the podium, ready to perform, she would observe them watching her, and her heart would swell with pride and thanksgiving that her adopted family took the time to come and hear her sing.

When the father-daughter banquet was scheduled for Irene's senior year of high school, she told William that she was invited to be the featured singer and asked if he would escort her to the banquet. He said he was too busy, though Irene knew that he could have made the time if he had wanted to.

She came home with a sore heart. Bob noticed her somber mood and asked what was wrong. She told him that she had no one to take her to the banquet, then with shy hope she said, "Pops, can you take me?"

Big tears gathered in his eyes, "Sure I will Irene. I'd love to take you to the father-daughter banquet." He gave her a big hug and her heart leapt with joy.

"Do you have a nice dress to wear?"

"No, Pops," she answered.

"Then let's get in the car and go buy you one." She could hardly believe her ears.

They climbed in the old Bonneville and drove downtown. He took her to a nice clothing store and waited patiently while she tried on dress after dress, passing judgment on each selection. Ultimately he decided on a pale blue dress with a high collar and long pleated sleeves. She looked stunning.

"We'll take it," he said, and he paid $47 for the dress.

At the banquet, Irene sang four or five songs and received enthusiastic applause for her performance. Then the Master of Ceremonies invited Irene to introduce her father. With joy and pride she presented Bob. He stood and received the honor.

These random acts of kindness were the only events that kept Irene's faith alive. She started to realize once again that good things could come from the hand of God. So even when her heart was hardened, angry and hurt with Him, the caring and understanding from Bob and Myrna encouraged her fledging faith.

Later that year Irene participated in the Miss Clatsup County pageant. She was a favorite, relatively well known for her singing in the community. She won the talent portion with little problem, but when the final ballots were tabulated, Irene took second runner-up. She was puzzled by this result, as the talent points represented 60 percent of the total score.

She mulled over her disappointment and pondered why she had not done better in the pageant. Not only were her talent points high, but she was approached by a modeling agency in Portland after the pageant to pursue that type of career. This supported her knowledge that she was no longer an ugly duckling, but a lovely young lady.

Finally, she approached a woman who had been involved with both the choreography and judging of the pageant. She asked why she had not done better. The woman hesitated, then apparently decided to tell Irene the truth. She told her that the person chosen to win the pageant had to represent the community, which meant that a certain amount of politics was involved in the decision. She said that there had been a three-way tie for first place, and that the tie had been broken based on the family background of each contestant.

"They know about the alcoholism and lack of stability in your family, Irene. And they know about the fire. They could not choose somebody like you to represent the community." Irene was astonished.

The woman continued, trying to be kind, but honest.

"Look Irene. Try again next year when you're in college. Maybe there will be more distance between you and your family's reputation. I'm really sorry this happened."

Toward the middle part of Irene's senior year Myrna was diagnosed with uterine cancer and had major surgery. During those months Irene took care of their house. Bob and Scott shared this burden. The men would scrub the floors and vacuum, so that not all the work depended on Irene. Myrna had cobalt treatments, still experimental at the time, which took a tremendous toll on the patient. Irene helped care for her.

Although Bob and Myrna still supported Irene in every way, their attention was understandably more focused during this time on Myrna's health. Inevitably, some of Irene's old loneliness returned.

Irene had one problem with Chris as a boyfriend. In high school he secretly drank, keeping this knowledge from his parents. But Irene was aware of his habit and had a wary nervousness about his potential as an alcoholic. She was more than conscious of the life-wrenching problems produced by this indulgence.

When Chris came home for visits from college, it was obvious that he had increased his drinking, not knowing where he was at times, driving the car while intoxicated, and disappearing for long hours. Irene was very concerned and unhappy with these developments.

She confronted him one evening when he picked her up for a date. They sat in the high school parking lot in his parents' green GMC pickup as the conversation grew more and more intense until both of them were shouting at the top of their voices.

Irene accused him of hanging around with the wrong crowd and being influenced by dead-beat friends. He did not attend his classes regularly and then complained that he wasn't doing well at school. She said to herself, looking at his faced flushed with anger at her accusations, "I will never marry an alcoholic."

At the end of the argument, they broke up.

Chris took Irene home, and she carefully controlled her face as she went to her room, where she allowed herself to feel the complete despair of the breakup. She was broken-hearted that he thought drinking was more important than their relationship.

He returned to college, and she realized that the breakup was "for good" when he refused to attend her high school graduation. At least Bob and Myrna were there.

Irene now focused her attention on a career in music. She applied to Linfield College in McMinnville, Oregon, and, after an extensive audition, she received a full four-year scholarship that covered all of her tuition, fees, books, room and board. Her only contribution would be her clothing and necessities.

Now it seemed her path was set, but so was her heart. She still stung from Chris's rejection and from the loss of hope to have a marriage, home, and family man who did not drink. She had tried to be a good person, keeping herself clean and decent, and it had gotten her nowhere.

Now, with Chris out of her life and away for the summer, she tried a new approach to life, one she had seen amply demonstrated by Evelyn and Shirley. In a warped desire for attention she decided to try "the fast lane."

She dated boys that she once would not have even considered. If the community thought she was a bad girl, then she would show them what a bad girl she could be. By the middle of summer, she was pregnant.

She confided in a girlfriend who had also gotten pregnant, and was first advised to have a pregnancy test, then to have an abortion. She went to her doctor who confirmed her condition.

For several days she pondered about what to do, wondering where she could get advice. She thought about her future, the four-year college scholarship, her still active desire to marry Chris if he straightened out his life. She had an intense motive and drive to put music first instead of anything else. And there was the tremendous fear that she had let everybody down.

She felt like she might never get back on track, to be what she wanted to be, finishing college, having a career. She considered the intense embarrassment of telling Chris's parents about the baby. It would be even worse since Chris was not the father.

And finally, she prayed.

Almighty God knows the hearts and minds of His children, and He knew hers. When Irene eventually turned to Him for guidance, for an affirmation of her actions, her mind was already made up. For fear of the many ramifications of carrying the child and giving birth out of wedlock, she decided to have an abortion. She was so firm in her decision that she convinced herself that she had total peace about it.

When she prayed, in this atmosphere, she convinced herself that she had His blessing, that it was okay to proceed with the abortion. Her friend called and made arrangements for the procedure, and Irene was left trying to come up with the $150 fee.

She finally gathered the courage to talk to William about her difficulties. After a long and exhausting discussion, he gave her the money. Irene asked William's girlfriend Ramona to drive her to Portland, and she reluctantly agreed.

On the day of the appointment, Ramona picked up Irene on the pretense of a shopping trip to the city. As they drove along, she gently tried to talk Irene out of her plan. She knew it was a mistake and believed that Irene would regret her action for all her life. But Irene was unyielding in her determination. She tried to explain that she did not want to be like the other people in Astoria that were drunk and had no place to go. Their whole lives were wrapped up in bars and having children outside of marriage. She just didn't think she could do it.

Ramona drove her to the Lovejoy Clinic, and there they sat together waiting for Irene to be called. There were other women in the waiting area filling out the necessary forms. Irene had been coached and warned by her girlfriend about the "acceptable" answers to the questions.

Then she was taken into a hallway with benches along both sides. She sat there waiting with six other women while a short, thin, older nurse spoke to them in brisk, no-nonsense tones about the procedures. Eventually, they were taken as a group into a large room where they all disrobed together. There was no privacy. It was like a scene from Auschwitz. They put on hospital gowns and crawled up on tall hospital beds.

In the quiet of the clinic, low sobs could be heard. And as the waiting continued, each of the six women gave way to her own private lament, tears wetting their anguished faces.

On Irene's left was a housewife. She told Irene that she had two other kids and she wanted this baby very badly.

"Why are you doing this?" Irene asked.

"My husband doesn't want any more children. He'll divorce me if I have this child," she sobbed, then turned over, weeping in despair.

Irene looked at the other women. One was obviously a prostitute. She said that it was her third abortion.

Irene told her vehemently that this was her first and her only abortion, that she would never do this horrible thing again. Even in this atmosphere of devastation, she was determined to go through with it. Ramona came in from the waiting room and asked, one final time, if Irene was sure she wanted the abortion.

"Irene, if you change your mind, I can open this window right here and we can jump right out and go home. It'll be fine, really!" She begged Irene to leave with her.

"No, I'm going to do it," she answered. Ramona shook her head sadly and went back to the waiting room.

The nurse came in and, one by one, inserted a reed-like object to dilate the cervix. She moved from patient to patient, absorbed in her work, oblivious to the emotional devastation around her. Shortly, the women were called, one by one, and taken into the next room where the abortion was performed.

They went into a small room with an examination table. The nurse took Irene's blood pressure, but administered no anesthetic or drug. In a few minutes a man entered and introduced himself as Dr. Newman. He shook her hand and began to work. The nurse asked if Irene was okay, then they turned on the machinery, which looked and acted very much like a vacuum cleaner. The doctor pushed hard on Irene's stomach and after two minutes of intense pressure the procedure was completed.

They rolled her bed into another room where she rested briefly. Then she put on her clothes and left with Ramona. They drove in silence back to Astoria. She went in and told Bob and Myrna that she thought she had the flu. And after a few days she was physically recovered.

Irene decided that she would think of the incident as a sacrifice that she had made for music, for herself, and for the other people around her. She determined that she had made the best decision possible, that she would start college with her head high, looking to a bright future.

Unfortunately, her spirit did not follow her strong will. Almost immediately she started having trouble sleeping. She would wake in a cold sweat from some nagging nightmare, just outside her conscious memory. In the daytime, she relived the revolting memories of that day in Portland.

In private, she cried endlessly, grieving over the death of her baby, praying that it was all a bad dream. Now that it was over, she felt the deadening weight of these memories like a millstone hanging around her neck. And she wondered whether — even if Chris stopped drinking — she could ever be worthy of his trust and love again.

In September, Myrna drove her to McMinnville for college, and she again tried to set her mind on the business of education. She worked hard at her lessons and tried her very best to concentrate on her studies. But she was obsessed with thoughts about the abortion. She went to a college counselor once a week, trying to get herself back on track.

"You're a good person," he told her. "It's okay. God can forgive you — even for taking a life."

She listened and tried to believe, but the memory of it was like a broken record, playing over and over again. Babies would cry and she would flash back to that horrible day. Maybe God could forgive her, but she could not forgive herself.

As autumn grew colder and winter approached, the Gideons International group came to the college, handing out Bibles and counseling the students. Irene went to one of their tables to talk with one of the men. He gave her a Bible and a tract.

The next day, the Gideons were still on her mind. She found herself in a conversation with another student about faith. She told the young man that she was a Christian, but she had gotten off course. He smiled at her gently and reminded her that God still loved her, that He wanted her to come back to Him. The young man's kind eyes and loving words touched her heart. And as they prayed together, they shared a sweet moment which gently drew Irene back into the arms of her loving Heavenly Father.

She began to read the Bible, and with God's help, she began to understand the words. She attended the Baptist church. Slowly her feelings of despair lifted, and she began to be happy.

During Christmas vacation, Irene visited Chris. They talked for a long time, and she told him how she had drifted away from the Lord, but was ready to become stronger in her faith. Chris talked about the Lord, but was not as certain about where he stood. Then Irene took a deep breath and told him about the abortion, praying in her heart that he would not reject her.

For awhile there was only silence. Then he took her gently in his arms.

"Even if it wasn't my baby, I probably would have married you, because I love you that much," he said. "If we could rewind history, I hope you would feel good enough to come and talk to me. We probably would have gotten married and no one would have ever known, except you and me."

And then Chris cried over the loss of the child.

In February, Chris came up from college to visit Irene. By now he had almost stopped drinking and seemed to be getting his life in order. They spent wonderful times together and started to talk about the future.

"Come on Irene. I want to get you something," he said one afternoon.

They went downtown to a jewelry store and started looking at engagement rings. They settled on a beautiful diamond, and he bought it on the spot. "There, now do you feel better?" he asked.

"Yes, Chris," she answered, still not quite satisfied.

"Okay, let's get married in August, before school starts."

"Yes, Chris," she said, waiting.

"How about August fourth," he bludgeoned on.

"That's fine, Chris." She gritted her teeth.

By then, they were walking across the tennis courts of Linfield College, holding hands when he suddenly stopped.

"Wait a minute, wait a minute." She looked at him expectantly. He got down on one knee and said.

"Irene, I have loved you, and I will always love you. I want you to be my wife and be with me forever."

"You really asked me!" she laughed.

"I thought I'd better make this official," he said.

When she said "yes," he kissed her.

During that summer Chris worked at the plywood mill and

Irene at the nursing home and at the cannery to save money for a nice wedding. Bob and Myrna were less than enthusiastic about the marriage, since Chris had once been so involved with partying and drinking. Irene decided to give up her scholarship. She had put music first for so long and in such a powerful way, it was doubtful that she could put a husband first in her priorities. There seemed to be many strikes against the marriage. But they persisted with their plans and Irene moved back in with Evelyn when Chris returned home for summer break.

On their wedding day, August 4, 1973, Irene kicked Laura and Ruth out of their bed in Evelyn's house and told them to get up. She put on her bathrobe, a Christmas gift from Bob and Myrna, and went into the kitchen to prepare breakfast for the seven people cramped into the small apartment in preparation for the wedding. She deeply resented this, yet not even that injustice could mar the joy and beauty of her marriage day.

Irene wore a beautiful wedding dress that her grandmother Ada bought years before and saved carefully in a trunk. As a child, Ada would take Irene to the attic to examine the dress of thick imported satin with French lace on the bodice extending nearly to the knees. Irene had dreamed of being married in this special gown which weighed at least 20 pounds, had more than 100 buttons down the back and arms, and had an eight-foot train.

In this dress, Irene's Cinderella story came true. More than 400 people, friends of Bob and Myrna and numerous people from the community who had heard Irene sing, attended the wedding. It was a magical and beautiful moment.

As Irene walked down the aisle, tears streamed down Chris's face. He took her hand and said, "I've never seen and I'll never see anything more beautiful than how you look today."

But in Irene's mind, shadowing the perfection of this occasion, were two intrusive memories. She ached with the desire to know her real father, to have him walk down the aisle with her, to know his love and approval. And second was the fear that if her grandmother only knew about her past sins, she would never have let her wear that special gown.

MARRIAGE

Hear, O Israel; the Lord our God is one Lord — the only Lord. And you shall love the Lord your God with all your [mind and] heart, and with your entire being, and with all your might. And these words, which I am commanding you this day, shall be [first] in your own mind and heart; [then] You shall whet and sharpen them, so as to make them penetrate, and teach and impress them diligently upon the [minds and] hearts of your children, and shall talk of them when you sit in your house, and when you walk by the way, and when you lie down and when you rise up. And you shall bind them as a sign upon your hand, and they shall be as frontlets (forehead bands) between your eyes. And you shall write them upon the doorposts of your house and on your gates.

Deuteronomy 6:4-9 AMP

But who can endure the day of His coming? Who can stand when He appears? For He will be like a refiner's fire or a launderer's soap. He will sit as a refiner and purifier of silver; He will purify the Levites and refine them like gold and silver. Then the Lord will have men who will bring offerings in righteousness, and the offerings of Judah and Jerusalem will be acceptable to the Lord, as in days gone by, as in former years.

Malachi 3:2-4 NIV

111

Chris and Irene honeymooned in Victoria, B.C. in a beautiful old hotel surrounded by acres of manicured flower gardens. They rode in a horse drawn carriage and ate at elegant restaurants. Now, instead of a slave, Irene felt like a queen, having the very best of everything.

They returned to Astoria and moved into a small apartment to begin their lives together. They had a wonderful time riding the motorcycle and beachcombing for sand dollars and trinkets from the ocean. They started going to the Methodist church, sang in the choir, and Chris taught a Sunday School class.

As their love deepened, they began to think of starting a family. Chris and Irene talked about children many times, but in the hesitancy of this new marriage, Irene hid from Chris her deep, gnawing fear. She wondered if the unspeakable things that Grandpa Jess had done to her would prevent her from having children. And she heard on the radio that women who had an abortion sometimes could not conceive again. The deep guilt over her unspeakable offense reinforced this fear. She lay awake in the night, worrying and praying.

One night, eight months later, while Chris was at work, Irene remembered what she learned from her Sunday school teacher: "When you want to get in touch with God, you first ask for forgiveness, and then give Him your request. As you give Him your request, hold your hands out, cupping them together and lifting them up to God."

Sitting in the bathtub with the hot water streaming around her body, she lifted her cupped hands to God and asked His forgiveness for having the abortion. As she asked, guilt and sorrow poured over her — and her heart broke with the magnitude of her sin.

As tears streamed down her face, she said, "The first child You gave me, I did not care for. I can see why You wouldn't want to give me another one. But I am so sorry, God. I wasn't willing to hear Your voice, and I went my own way. Please forgive me."

She prayed fervently, meaning every word. Then a peaceful feeling came over her. She felt like a rope had been tied around her chest for all those months, and it was now loosened.

The feeling of freedom was so unexpected, so wonderful. A smile lit her face.

One month later she was pregnant, and she told Chris it was better than getting a million dollars. They laughed together, filled with joy. She talked to her flat stomach and rubbed it, ecstatic about the baby and thanking God, with great delight, for His answer to her prayers. But the larger miracle was the healing in her spirit.

One day, while Irene waited on the Lord to produce His miracle baby, she received a phone call from the hospital. Chris had been working additional hours at the plywood mill and was operating a new machine. It had a conveyor belt that ran the wood into a pressure chamber and compressed the lumber under 800 pounds of pressure to remove moisture and begin the drying process. As he started the machine, his heavy army coat became entangled with the chain and he was pulled into the compressor. He screamed as he was drawn under the massive dryer roller which smashed his right arm clear up to his neck before the automatic shut-off stopped the machine just short of his head. It took the men 30 minutes, using sledge hammers and wedges to lever some of the 800-pound weight off his right arm, in an attempt at maintaining his circulation. Then the welders took two hours to cut him out of the rollers.

They rushed Chris to the hospital, and finally someone called Irene. The doctors told her: "Be prepared. There's a 75 percent chance that he will not come home with his arm."

She was devastated.

"Oh God," she prayed, "It's his right arm. How will he be able to write or do normal things again?" She called their friends at the Methodist church, and many people joined in her prayer to spare Chris' arm and allow him to return to normal life.

Ten days later he went home, still in possession of his right arm which hung uselessly in the bandages. The bones in his arm miraculously not had been broken, but the muscle, tissue, and nerves were crushed, probably beyond repair. He began therapy immediately, struggling to bring the arm back to life.

It was during this time, when his arm began to heal and Irene's stomach swelled with new life, that the Lord began to work in Chris. They read *The Living Bible* together, and pulled closer to their Maker in these hard times. And as they read, Irene realized that Chris had never accepted Jesus as his personal Savior.

God was wooing him during his healing after the accident. For five months, he had no feeling in his hand. In therapy, they put a brace on his arm and moved the muscles with electric shock. But they could discern no nerve activity in the arm. They continued to pray, and God answered their prayer. In another few months the muscles in his arm were fully restored and he regained full use of his arm and hand. It was a miracle!

In October, Chris returned to work at the plywood mill, aware in his heart that only God could have healed him. He and Irene continued to read the Bible each day and grow to know the Lord more intimately.

In November, they attended a three-day Lay Witness Mission meeting at the Methodist church. Irene sat miserably, eight months pregnant, through the hours of meetings, watching with great intensity as Chris opened his heart to these people of God. He admitted that he did not really know what it meant to be a follower of Jesus, but that he felt the Lord was drawing him to a clearer understanding of what it meant to be a Christian.

On that Sunday morning, just before noon, the Lay Witness Missionaries in the Methodist church gave an altar call. The congregation rose to sing "How Great Thou Art," and a missionary stood up front waiting for people to come and accept Jesus as Savior.

As Irene watched, the Lord spoke to her, "Go down there, Irene."

She thought, "Why, Lord? Service is almost over, and I already know You. Besides, Chris hates this song, and he'll be mad if I go down there and drag this out any longer."

"Irene, you know Me, and you can hear My voice. You know when I'm telling you to do something," He continued.

"But I'm eight months pregnant, Lord. I'll look like a weevil waddling down there."

"No one is going to go down to that altar unless you do. If you obey me in this, both your husband and your mother-in-law will be saved. Later your whole family will be saved. And other people will be saved because of this one time of obedience. A lot of the other people do not hear Me when I talk to them. But you know My voice. Now you listen and go do what I asked you to do. Please go, Irene."

Her heart responded to His gentle voice, and she awkwardly made her way out of the choir loft, around the piano, in front of the organ, in front of the whole congregation, and clumsily knelt at the altar. For a long time, nothing happened.

In her mind, Irene continued to pray, "Okay God, I'm here. You know I want to live my life better for You now that I know what it is to be a Christian."

And God answered, "Irene, I have kept you for this day, that you would really come to know me. Now watch what I can do through your obedience."

Gradually, one by one, people joined her at the altar. As she continued to kneel, Chris' aunt and uncle came down, followed by three or four strangers. Then Irene looked up to find Chris' mother Myrna at her side, rededicating her life to the Lord. They held each other and wept tears of joy.

Chris waited, impatiently, for this emotional scene to end. He detested the song "How Great Thou Art." He thought that Irene's going down front had lengthened the service, which he planned to discuss with her later.

He waited and waited, and with the song droning on and on, it seemed to take forever. Then the thought popped into his mind, "Look at those women down there crying. Don't you think you better go and console them? They're making fools of themselves."

"That's a good idea," he thought. I'll go down and take them out of here. So he went down to "console" their crying and take them home. He walked out of the choir loft, passing in front of the same piano and organ — but as he approached the altar, God broke his heart.

Chris fell to his knees and began weeping from the depths of his heart as the Holy Spirit overwhelmed him. As God filled his heart with the knowledge of the reality of Jesus Christ, he began to pray out loud: "Jesus I want you as Lord of my life. I need you. I wish I could have known You before. Oh, Jesus, I want to lead a better life for You."

They all wept together, thanking the Lord for the changes He had made in their lives.

On that Sunday night, there was a follow-up meeting for the Lay Witnesses, and Chris announced there would be Bible study at their home the following evening.

Monday night came, and 30 people crowded into the small apartment and began to read and study the Word of God:

> *If thou shalt confess with thy mouth the Lord Jesus, and shalt believe in thine heart that God hath raised him from the dead, thou shalt be saved. For with the heart man believeth unto righteousness; and with the mouth confession is made unto salvation.*

Romans 9:9-10 KJV

The following months, they read the Bible, consuming it with great relish, like hungry people eating bread for the first time. It was a good time spiritually, but Irene was having increased physical problems as she neared the end of her pregnancy.

In December, she developed shingles on her left side, accompanied by painful blisters. Then her doctor diagnosed toxemia and her blood pressure shot up. She had terrible headaches and her vision began to fail. Within weeks, she lost her singing voice completely and with that, her identity as a musician. Her speaking voice was very hoarse and raspy. She slept most of the time.

The doctor planned for a Cesarean delivery. On the day Irene was scheduled for surgery, she went into labor, her blood pressure so high that the doctor thought she would lapse into a coma. She was deathly ill. Chris' mother sat for hours putting cool washcloths on her forehead and praying for her.

Evelyn came to the hospital. It was the first time they had seen her in months. Irene was touched that, though countless times before she had needed her mother and known nothing but neglect, Evelyn had come to help her in this desperate time. But her mother had come only to criticize.

"You're not having nearly as bad a time as Shirley did," she said, to Myrna's amazement, and then continued on with other rude comparisons. Irene heard everything from deep in her fevered mind. Myrna finally asked Evelyn to leave.

A few hours later, Irene gave birth to a healthy seven-pound, 11-ounce baby girl named Christy. After the delivery, Irene was sick and exhausted. She could not sleep. One day passed, and then another, and she remained haunted by insomnia. Two days later, when she returned home with the baby, she still had not slept at all. The next morning she wanted to nurse her new daughter, but Chris' mother did not approve. So Irene gave Christy a bottle, but was very disturbed at this unexpected intervention. As she sat, exhausted from the days without sleep, she dwelled on this intrusion. Her thoughts turned to fears. Maybe they were right. Maybe she couldn't ever be a good mother. Maybe she didn't deserve a baby because of her past.

In her extreme weariness these fears grew out of proportion. She became obsessed with anxieties. Now she heard another voice in her head, and it was not God. "How do you expect to have any success? Look at your family. Look at what you have done in your life. There is no God. Just denounce Him and go your own way. You'll hurt your children just like every other generation of your family before you. You can't trust yourself with a baby."

But her greatest fear, increasing with each day of sleeplessness, was that of dying. She felt so physically ill and believed that no one was taking her infirmity seriously. She was sure that she was going to perish.

And because of the unforgiveness in her heart — toward her mother, toward her grandfather, toward her family for blaming her for the fire, and most of all, toward herself — these accusations took root. Her behavior became erratic. She began talking to herself and throwing things around the house. Chris watched with growing concern.

On the evening of the seventh day of complete sleeplessness, she lay down, wide awake, praying for sleep to relieve her. She felt so sick that she could not move. She laid there listening to her heart pounding and her head throbbing, feeling like she was going to die.

Suddenly the room went dark, and she felt herself leave her body. She looked down from the ceiling and saw herself on the bed. Then something pulled her through the ceiling. She watched as the earth grew smaller and stars flew by at an incredible speed. She was pulled gently into a tunnel with lights brighter than daylight at the other end.

She heard the voice of the Lord saying, "It is not your time to die yet. I'm going to send you back."

She listened in awe.

"You have so many things to do for Me yet. I cannot have you come home now."

And suddenly she was back in her body, catching her breath and feeling alive again. She was so excited about this amazing experience that it lifted her spirits for the next several days. But still, she could not sleep.

Spiritually, she had been uplifted, but physically she was in bad shape. In the following days she again became convinced that she was going to die. Hour after hour her anxiety grew and the assurance she had felt from the vision faded. She constantly felt the deep pounding beat of her heart, and it was frightening. Her hands and eyes burned with soreness, and she had severe chest pains which seemed to almost stop her breathing.

On the tenth sleepless day, she rose from another night spent tossing and turning, her mind screaming from lack of sleep. She fed Christy her bottle, then went into the bathroom to wash her face. As she stood looking at her haggard appearance in the mirror, she was overcome with despair and cried out to the Lord.

"Jesus, I know I'm going to die. Please make the assurance to me that I really will go to heaven. Show me how I can trust You." Again the memory of her past had convinced her that only the fires of hell awaited her.

Suddenly she heard a gentle voice say, "You're going to be okay," and felt herself being picked up bodily from the bathroom. And then she was in the living room, down the long hallway.

She sat in surprise as the far wall of the room seemed to open up like a drive inn movie screen. She saw a man kneeling against large rocks, and recognized Him as Jesus praying in the Garden of Gethsemane. And as she watched she heard His voice praying for her.

"God, forgive her and accept her. Don't let the enemy take her life." The Lord allowed her to hear the words that He was praying for her. Jesus Christ was personally interceding with Almighty God on her behalf.

"I accept her as My child. She will belong to no other. And I will teach her how to forgive."

Then Jesus stood up and turned toward Irene, but she could not see His face clearly.

"You're going to be all right. I have fought the fight for you, and the battle is won," He continued. "Even though it will be hard in the days to come, you're going to be all right. Though Satan wants to sift you like wheat, I have prayed for you."

Then she felt herself lifted again and set gently back in the bathroom. She looked in the mirror and said, "Wow! To see a vision once in a lifetime is enough."

Her legs were shaky and she felt weak. She remembered that as a child she asked God to give her a vision of Himself and now, shaken to her very being, she was glad He had not granted her request. She understood that it would have overwhelmed her. But now, when she needed it most, He had answered her prayer.

Later that day, her doctor came to the house to check on the baby. In her excitement she made the mistake of telling him about the vision the Lord had given her. He listened to her, then talked to Chris, who told him about her physical ailments, the burning in her hands and eyes, chest pain, and her erratic behavior. The doctor said it was just anxiety, but he took Irene out to his car and drove her to the hospital. She was admitted to the lock-up psychiatric room of the hospital.

As Irene continued to share her heavenly vision with the people around her, she was unaware that this behavior took the attention of hospital personnel away from the source of her physical problem, her lack of sleep. They took no blood tests, nor did they give her any other examination to determine the reason for her insomnia. She was too tired to think clearly and did not see that her rambling, excited chatter about Jesus only strengthened their conviction that she had gone over the edge of insanity.

They administered tranquilizers, trying to calm her. Irene soon realized that she was in serious trouble.

As she prayed silently in her cell, again the Lord spoke to her: "I'm going to show you how to forgive, Irene. It's hard, and it hurts, but you will learn it. I'll bring up situations in your life and teach you how to do it, through My Word and through My Self. I have too much work for you to do in the future to not to repair you emotionally and spiritually. I will make you into a whole person. I will give you specific scriptures. Like a doctor gives a prescription to a patient, I will show you what in My Word I want you to read."

"Lord, why do You speak to me so clearly, in words in my head, just like a conversation? Maybe I am really crazy. Maybe I make all this up in my own mind."

"I speak to you because, as a child, you prayed and asked to hear My voice. I have answered your prayer. I know your difficulties in reading, especially reading My Word, but if you listen I will continue to talk to you. Remember, I will instruct you as a father, and I will never leave you fatherless. You are not crazy; it is My voice you hear."

And so she waited, through her allergic reaction to the drugs and through her impatience with the medical personnel. She eventually began to sleep for a few hours at a time.

On her third day in the lock-up unit, she was gently awakened by the Lord.

"Now don't talk about the tunnel, or the vision or Me, because they don't understand, and they're going to think you're crazy," the Lord said. "I will keep you as the apple of my eye."

"What does that mean, Jesus?" she asked.

"When you get so close to someone that you can see your own reflection in their eyes, that is how close I will keep you to Me," he explained. "And you will be okay. You're going to get through this. When they come in, do not talk about anything but Chris and the baby. Nothing else."

When the nurses and counselors came around, she obeyed the Lord and made no mention of these things. She asked to see Christy and Chris, and told them she just wanted to go home and be with her family. She apologized and said that she recognized that she had been a victim of post-partum depression. They asked her questions to test her, and she carefully answered them. And then they released her.

On the way home the Lord spoke to her again.

"There will be many things that we will have to deal with, Irene. But just lay them aside, and you and I will go through them, and it will be okay. I will show you how to put them into perspective. It will take time, but we'll do it. You'll make it."

And that night she slept.

In the next several weeks, Irene concentrated on caring for Chris and Christy. Many of her fears remained, and she was burdened by a lack of knowledge about doing things for the baby. But Jesus was so real to her now that she would look to Him first for guidance. As she opened the Word each morning He gave her specific scriptures for each day, such as:

> *So do not fear, for I am with you; do not be dismayed, for I am your God. I will strengthen you and help you. I will uphold you with my righteous right hand. All who rage against you will surely be ashamed and disgraced; those who oppose you will be as nothing and perish. Though you search for your enemies, you will not find them. Those who wage war against you will be as nothing at all. For I am the Lord, your God, who takes hold of your right hand and says to you, Do not fear; I will help you.*

Isaiah 41:10-13 NIV

And since she had no preconceptions of the "proper" questions to ask God, she asked Him about everything — how to give Christy a bath, how to dress her, how to tell if she was too warm or too cold. And He answered these questions specifically, in her spirit. He reminded her to carefully dry between the baby's toes, to prevent chaffing. He told her to be careful of the soft spot on her head. He showed her how to clip Christy's tiny nails so she wouldn't scratch herself.

She remembered taking her mother's hand down the steep steps as a child in Hood River and realized that He was leading her step by step in learning to care for her precious child.

The Lord whispered in her ear, "Now listen, Irene. Every day I'm going to show you, as a father would show his own child, how to do things. I'll teach you how to be a mom. Don't worry about haunting memories of your past. All those old things are going to fall away, just like leaves off a tree. As they are falling, you'll understand many more things, and everything will be put in order."

And then He said, "Now, I have given you Christy, and I will help you to take care of her so you won't do the things that your mother did and fall into those traps that the enemy would set for you. But when you do, I'll be there to show you how to get out."

And so began part of the process of healing. Day after day, He would cause memories to surface, incidents Irene did not even remember happening to her. He would bring them up and show them to her, then heal them. Precept on precept and day after day the Lord renewed her mind by the cleansing of His Word:

> *Behold I send a messenger and he shall prepare the way before me. And the Lord, whom ye seek shall suddenly come in his temple even the messenger of the covenant whom ye delight in. Behold, he shall come, saith the Lord of Hosts. But who shall abide in the day of his coming, and who shall stand when he appeareth, for he is like a refining fire and like fuller's soap. And he shall sit as a refiner and purify the silver and he shall purify the sons of Levi and purge them as gold and silver. And they shall offer unto the Lord an offering of righteousness. And they shall offer to Judah and to Jerusalem and be pleasant unto the Lord as in the days of old, as in the former years.*
>
> Malachi 3:1-5 KJV

And then He showed her a picture of how He wanted to restore the brokenness in her life. "Your memory is like a dresser," the Lord told her, "a dresser full of clothes that are dirty, torn and unclean — clothes that are too small and don't fit."

"When you open a drawer, unseemly things fall out. There are secret places of hurt and abuse, and you feel like that is your whole life — dirty, ugly things. But I want to open up the drawer, take out the clothing and wash them. Some of them we need to throw away, but some we need to keep. And so we wash and mend them, iron them carefully and fold them neatly, placing them back into the drawer."

As they began to work through the long and difficult process toward wholeness, He gave her another "prescription":

> *For God has not given us a spirit of timidity — of cowardice, of craven and cringing and fawning fear — but [He has given us a spirit] of power and of love and of calm and well-balanced mind and discipline and self-control.*
>
> II Timothy 1:7 AMP

Although her sleep was still not normal, there were now nights when she did rest and wake up refreshed. And one night, God gave her a spiritual dream, to again reassure Irene that her place with Him was secure.

She dreamed that Jesus called her by name and took her by the hand, leading her to the front of a giant hall and up to a huge podium made of marble and wood. On the podium was an enormous book with a black cover and white pages. As she watched He opened the book, gesturing for her to look inside. There, in big bold, red script, was her name written in capital letters.

Jesus said, "Your name is written here. Do you see the mark by it?"

"Yes," she answered, timidly, noting the symbol in a shape like an asterisk.

"That mark means you are My child."

She looked again, making sure that the mark was right by her name. Then she noticed that underneath her name and across on the other page, there were large wide dark marks. It looked as though portions of the ledger had been deleted with a wide black marker, leaving broad stripes on the heavy parchment.

"What are these, Jesus?" she asked, pointing to the blackened rectangles on the page.

"Those are the people who did not accept Me."

"You mean everybody's name is in this book?"

"Yes. And when they die and they haven't accepted Me, I have to blot their name from the Book of Life."

She looked in His face, shocked by the depth of grief in His voice. They stood in silence for a moment, then He took her hand and turned away from the book.

"I am so glad that you're My child," He said. When He removed His hand, there was a white stone in her palm. She examined the rock and saw writing there.

"That's your new name, Irene." And although she later did not remember the heavenly name, she knew that it meant the very essence of tranquillity — that her future was in peace.

As she walked out of the great hall, she heard a multitude of angels singing to God, praising Him as they received the news that someone on earth had accepted the Lord Jesus. She walked on a red plush carpet and on both sides of the path were ropes used to hold back the crowds. Behind the ropes were hundreds of people and hordes of angels jumping up and down and screaming and yelling and shouting joyfully. And as she walked on toward the great throne sitting high on the dais, the Lord God Almighty stood up and waited for her. As she reached His side, He said, "This is for you, My daughter."

She was completely confounded that Jesus Christ was standing up for her.

When Irene woke the next morning, as if to seal the memory of her wonderful dream, the Lord gave her a verse for the day:

> *He who is able to hear, let him listen to and heed what the Spirit says to the assemblies (the churches). To him who overcomes (who conquers) I will give to eat of the manna that is hidden, and I will give him a white stone, with a new name engraved on the stone which no one knows or understands except he who receives it.*

> Revelations 2:17 AMP

She had never seen this scripture before.

On another morning, God began to deal with Irene about the abortion. The first thing He told her was that in His great mercy, He understood her pain and confusion.

"You don't have to be fearful about that anymore, Irene. You have a little boy here with Me in heaven, and his name is Joseph." Irene could barely grasp the wonder of this miracle. Her mind was infused with new assurance.

"And his second name is Samuel, isn't it?" She suddenly knew about her son.

And the Lord said, "That's right. He's here with me. You know you did wrong then, but that's okay. I can redeem that sin. He's in heaven with me, and I'm taking care of him. And he's here with Sammy and David and they already know him. So don't you worry. He has somebody up here to be with."

Irene was overwhelmed with a sense of forgiveness for the abortion, for her lack of faith, for the times she had parted from the Lord and gone her own way.

She wept tears of joy as the burden of her guilt lifted away.

In the evenings, Chris would come home from the plywood factory and sit with Christy in the big old rocking chair, singing to her and playing with her. As Irene watched this tender scene, she could hardly believe how her life was being turned around. Tears welled up in her eyes. Now she was beginning to understand joy, from glory to glory.

And all of us, as with unveiled face, [because we] continued to behold [in the Word of God] as in a mirror the glory of the Lord, are constantly being transfigured into His very own image in ever increasing splendor and from one degree of glory to another; [for this comes] from the Lord [Who is] the Spirit.

II Corinthians 3:18 AMP

One beautiful sunny day, on one of those rare occasions when it didn't rain in Astoria, the Lord told Irene to put Christy in the stroller and go for a nice walk in the sunshine. Irene already had her day mentally lined out and did not particularly want to pack the bottles, diapers, crackers and all the other necessary paraphernalia for the baby. But He was gently insistent.

"Okay, Lord. Well, where are we going? This feels weird."

He responded, "No, it'll be all right. It's a nice sunny day and we can just go for a walk, and you and I can have a nice talk." And so he talked to her about Christy and the beauty of the day, nothing really out of the ordinary.

As she strolled down the sidewalk, watching Christy waving her hands at the people, Irene asked the Lord, "Where are we going?"

"To the hospital." A chill came over her. She remembered the horror of the lock-up room on the third floor.

"Uh, do I have to go back there?"

And He said, "You're not going back in the lock-up room. You're going to go there for something that I want you to do, to talk to somebody."

"All right. But I'm not going upstairs." She spoke honestly.

"That's all right. You just come with Me." She walked down the hall and into the last room at the end of the corridor. There were two ladies resting in their beds, the second one sobbing into her pillow. The bottom half of the sheet lay flat against the mattress on the right side. Her leg had been amputated.

"Hi, I'm Irene. I just felt like I was supposed to come and visit you. I know you don't know who I am, but I just thought it would be good if I came to see you," Irene stuttered, not knowing what to say.

The woman looked up in surprise. Irene continued talking about the beautiful day. Then she picked up Christy and let her sit on the bed with the sorrowful woman.

The woman's face brightened a bit as the happy child cooed and giggled. She reached out for the baby and held her, smiling at her joyful baby face.

Irene said, "Why are you so sad?"

"I'll never be able to walk again. Never be able to go outside again. Never do normal things again." Her story poured out in a mass of pain and fear.

"Not one person on this earth cares about me. The doctor said the operation wasn't enough. I have bone cancer, and it's spreading. And I'm so afraid to die."

Irene looked at the woman's face, wracked with pain and sorrow, and her heart broke for this stranger.

"Do you know about heaven?" The woman considered the question carefully.

"Yes, but I don't know how to get there." And Irene began to tell her about heaven, about the visions and dreams the Lord had given her. She talked to her about the angels, and the great book, and the Lord God.

"In heaven, you'll have two legs and be able to run and walk. It'll be a great thing."

"Well, how do you get there? I don't know anything about these things."

So Irene shared with her about Jesus and having Him in her heart and that she would be able to go to heaven if she would just accept Him as her Lord and Savior. The woman reached out her hand to Irene.

"Please, show me how to pray." She took Irene's hand and repeated the sinner's prayer, asking Jesus into her heart. Two days later, she died.

During all these months, Irene had still not recovered her voice. Chris and his mother grew more and more concerned that this condition was permanent. So Irene went to see a new doctor

— and for the first time she was given a thyroid test which revealed levels so low that they were capable of inducing heart palpitations, depression, and a multitude of other afflictions. She was immediately put on medication and scheduled for a thyroid scan. The doctor diagnosed a substernal goiter, a tumor extending from her neck all the way down to below her sternum. The doctor told her she was lucky to be alive.

"Your vocal cords are white because of a lack of thyroid," he said. "You need to get to an endocrinologist immediately. You could die from this." He scheduled an appointment two days later with an endocrinologist.

Now, finally, she could be free of her fears of the lock-up ward. She was not crazy, she was ill. All those months of difficulty with her pregnancy, erratic behavior, and feeling so sick now made perfect sense. Her doctor scheduled her for surgery.

But the Lord had other plans. Before surgery, another scan was taken and the goiter had been completely healed. Irene remained on the thyroid medication and gradually began to feel strong and healthy. Slowly, her voice returned and again the Lord reassured her with His Word.

Chris and Irene bought a small house in Astoria. Irene was ecstatic. For the first time in her life she had her own home, a place of permanence where they could establish their family. They settled in and believed that their future lay in having a nice home and family there while Chris continued working at the plywood mill. But, again, God had other plans!

The first part of His plan was for Irene to have a clear conscience. He began teaching her how to forgive the people in her past by showing her scriptures such as:

Then came Peter to him, and said, Lord, how oft shall my brother sin against me, and I forgive him? till seven times? Jesus saith unto him, I say not unto thee, Until seven times: but, Until seventy times seven.

Therefore is the kingdom of heaven likened unto a certain king, which would take account of his servants. And when he had begun to reckon, one was brought unto him, which owed him ten thousand talents. But forasmuch as he had not to pay, his lord commanded him to be sold, and his wife, and children, and all that he had, and payment to be made. The servant therefore fell down, and worshipped him, saying, Lord, have patience with me, and I will pay thee all. Then the lord of that servant was moved with compassion, and loosed him, and forgave him the debt.

But the same servant went out, and found one of his fellow servants, which owed him a hundred pence: and he laid hands on him, and took him by the throat, saying, Pay me that thou owest. And his fellow servant fell down at his feet, and besought him, saying, Have patience with me, and I will pay thee all. And he would not: but went and cast him into prison, till he should pay the debt. So when his fellow servants saw what was done, they were very sorry, and came and told unto their lord all that was done.

Then his lord, after that he had called him, said unto him, O thou wicked servant, I forgave thee all that debt, because thou desiredst me: Shouldest not thou also have had compassion on thy fellow servant, even as I had pity on thee? **And his lord was wroth, and delivered him to the tormentors, till he should pay all that was due unto him. So likewise shall my heavenly Father do also unto you, if ye from your hearts forgive not every one his brother their trespasses.**

Matthew 18:21-35 KJV

The Lord showed Irene that there are three parts to forgiveness. First she should ask for forgiveness from God for the wrongs she has committed. Second, she needed to forgive other people for the wrongs done to her — and unless He directed her otherwise, she needed to tell those persons that she forgave them. Finally, she needed to forgive herself.

"Your debt toward Me was very great," He said to her, "and I forgave you every one. Now you must complete the process."

Irene took His words to heart, vowing to sit down and make a list of every person that had wronged her in her life. At first the choices were obvious: her mother for the abuse and for loving Shirley more than the other children, her step-father for not believing her about the fire, Nina for the fire and the death of her brother and nephew, her real father for abandoning her and her family in Alaska. On and on the list grew.

As the Holy Spirit continued to prod her, He told her that forgiveness was like an onion, with layers and layers that needed to be exposed and healed. He instructed her to pray for various people on her long list. Periodically, He woke her from sleep to pray for a person on the list, especially for her real father, Dwayne. However, she knew that the most important person on the list was Grandpa Jess, and that the Lord wanted her to confront him in person.

"If there is any way that you can confront him, face to face, you need to do it," the Lord told her.

"God, there is no way I can confront him. He scares me! He looks like the devil to me."

And God said, "And he always will until you resolve this. It's like a haunting memory that you'll never get rid of unless you confront him. You have to peel back this layer in order to be free. The odor of the onion brings a special kind of tears which will wash you clean forever of those old memories. I don't want the memories of that child abuse to haunt you anymore."

"Well, if You make the opportunity, then I'll do it. But I'm not pressing it, God, because it's just too scary to me. It's just like the devil's going to grab me around the neck and choke me."

Within a month, Chris and Irene received a call from William asking for their assistance. He needed to have a boat motor brought to him in Parkdale to Grandpa Jess' house so that he could do some repairs.

Irene cringed at the thought of this inevitable trip, yet she had no doubt that the Lord had set up this opportunity to speak to Grandpa Jess. She prayed fervently that her gut-wrenching fear of him would subside long enough for her to utter the words of forgiveness and fulfill her promise to the Lord to not hold her grandfather accountable any longer.

She and Chris stayed with Grandpa Jess and his new wife, but the hours were filled with trivial conversation and provided no opportunity for Irene to speak with him. As she and Chris prepared to leave, she prayed again, "Lord, if you want this to happen, you are going to have to make a way. We're ready to leave, and I cannot talk to him in front of anyone else — not even Chris."

As they walked to the car, Jess came out and offered to ride down to the station and put gas in their car for the return trip. Irene's stomach churned in anticipation. Her heart pounded in her ears.

They pulled into the station and Chris got out to fill the tanks. Irene turned around suddenly to confront her grandfather in the back seat and looked him full in the face. With her whole heart she said to him, "You know, Grandpa, I forgive you for all those things. Maybe you don't understand, but I forgive you."

He sucked in his breath with startled fear.

Irene continued, "It's not so much for your benefit, but for mine. I need to tell you this. Grandpa, I forgive you, because Jesus forgave me."

His face turned white, and he said nothing. Then Chris got back in the car.

Jess sat in the back seat with his eyes bulging with fear. He looked stunned that Irene had said the words, the releasing words, to the man that helped destroy her whole family.

They drove Jess back to the house and dropped him off. As they pulled away from this place of such foul and evil memories, Irene's heart lifted like a bird set free from a small and confining cage. Tears streamed down her face. She could feel the extreme pleasure of Almighty God that she was finally free of this bondage. The pain was totally gone.

One afternoon Chris and Irene drove to Portland so that Grandpa Ernie and Ada could see Christy. It was a wonderful time with family, and in the afternoon conversation Irene again asked her grandmother about her real father. Previously, Ada had avoided answering these questions, changing the subject abruptly. But this time, she told Irene about a man who lived in Whitson, Washington and who was married to Irene's aunt. She believed that he would know where Dwayne was living.

Irene was both excited and scared. On the return home, she and Chris called the man in Washington who gave them an address and phone number for her father.

She pondered about the many events that he had missed in

her life — her performances in music, her wedding, the birth of her child. She wondered if he would want to know her now.

With fear and trepidation she dialed the number and prayed, "Dear Father, please don't let him be upset. And please let him remember who I am."

When she reached him, they spoke tentatively at first.

"I thought that I would never speak to you again," he said, his voice breaking with tears.

She realized that he still loved her after all those years. They talked for a long time, birthing a new and healing relationship.

The next day Chris drove Irene to Longview, Washington to meet the father who had abandoned her family in Alaska so long ago, the father she had longed for and prayed for all those years. They introduced Dwayne to his new grandchild. Irene's heart sang as she experienced the healing of getting to know her father once again.

She told Dwayne that she had prayed for him for many years, and that sometimes the Lord awakened her in the middle of the night to pray for him. Dwayne looked at her quizzically and asked when this had occurred.

She thought for a minute, then told him it was a year before, in February.

"For four days in February, I prayed for you almost continuously."

"February?" he asked incredulously.

"Yes. Why?"

"February last year I had to stop drinking because I had a ruptured stomach. I was laying on the floor in my bathroom in a pool of blood. No one knew I was there. My neighbor broke in the apartment and found me there and saved my life. I don't even know how they knew anything was wrong. I was too weak to scream or yell. They saved my life."

He looked at Irene intensely. "I have wondered how they knew to help me. Now I know. It was your prayers." Tears spilled from his eyes and he came over and kissed Irene gently on her cheek.

That Sunday she invited Dwayne to listen to her sing at the church. And as she rose to sing "No One Ever Cared for Me Like Jesus," she realized that Dwayne was not among the 600 people in the congregation. He sat outside in his car. Having never entered a church before, he was unable to come inside, even to hear his own daughter sing. As the Lord had warned her, forgiveness was a hard and difficult thing to do.

In her hurt and rejection, Irene cried out to God, wanting to draw closer to Him than ever. She opened the Bible day after day, striving to read and understand the words of grace that waited just beyond her comprehension. She put her hands on the Bible and begged God to teach her how to read and understand His Word. Chris would read aloud to her and hearing the Word increased her faith and sustained her during these difficult months.

As the weeks went by, Irene and several other women started a Women's Aglow fellowship in the area. And as their fellowship grew they joined with other women to attend a retreat outside of Eugene, Oregon.

Women's Aglow, at that time, was white hot with the movement of the Holy Spirit. Many people operated in the gifts of the Spirit. People were prayed for and healed of both physical and spiritual maladies. It was a very exciting time for those churches.

At the retreat, a woman pulled Irene out of the audience and said she was going to pray for her. The woman, a total stranger, laid hands on Irene and prayed.

"No longer will you feel like an outcast. No longer will be unable to read. But I, the Lord your God, will give you insight and knowledge far above your reading ability. I come against fear and the impediment of reading skills."

Irene's mouth fell open as she listened to the powerful words of knowledge being spoken by the woman.

"No longer will your heading be illiterate. But your heading will be My daughter, My child, My precious one."

And as Irene listened, the prophecy continued and the Lord spoke to her concerning her father Dwayne.

"No longer do I want you to call Me God, or Father God. I want you to call Me Daddy. I am your Dad." As the woman finished speaking and moved on to another, Irene slipped out of the church and walked under a sky of brilliant stars.

The Lord continued, "Though your father and mother have forsaken you, I will bear you up and take you as My own child.

"I was there when you were born, and I waited for you just as a father waits expectantly for the birth of his first child. I watched you and took care of you even in your infancy. I was there when you were born. I greeted you with joy and expectation when you came into the world. I was happy that I could be your dad. Even before you were born you had a father, and that was Me. I cared for you. I spared your life from the neglect of your parents. I was there when you cried. I was there when you sang your first song, and I was pleased with you. I have never missed anything that you have done, ever.

"I felt your pain in all those situations. Everything that hurt you, hurt Me also. I have always been with you, and I'll always be with you. You will never be alone."

Irene heard and thought about the words and concepts pouring into her mind. But one question stood between herself and the acceptance of this love the Lord wanted to pour out on her.

"Why, God? If you have always been there, then why have all these things happened to me? You were there with Grandpa Jess, and you saw my mom beat us. Why?"

Her mind screamed out the questions in pain and confusion.

"Choices stand before each person, good and evil. I will not override that person's choice. I have sworn by My Word to give people free will, and I cannot go against My Word.

"Many of the bad things that have happened to you are the result of the people around you making evil choices. But I have limited the damage that they were allowed to inflict on you. I have spared the central part of your character that is My own daughter. And I will heal those wounded parts of you, that you will know that I am your Father and your God.

"Your future is bright. Don't worry about all that stuff."

In her spirit she knew the absolute truth of His words. Her heart responded to His healing touch.

The next day, she read the Bible with an open and powerful understanding. She still could not read a book or magazine — but the Word of God was no longer a closed book to her.

In the next few months, the Lord led them to the Philadelphia church in Hammond, Oregon, a charismatic nondenominational church where they were taught about the baptism in the Holy Spirit. Once baptized, the Lord took them out of the Methodist church and led them into a lay ministry at the Philadelphia church. They were in charge of all the music and home group activities for two-and-a-half years. The church exploded from a membership of 70 when they joined, to a membership of 600.

It was a powerful ministry. The Holy Spirit moved among His people, and as they prayed, He healed people of diseases and restored broken spirits. Before their very eyes a man's leg was lengthened three inches to match his other leg. He no longer had to wear a lift shoe. Another woman was healed of multiple sclerosis as Irene prayed for her. The healing was confirmed by the lady's doctors. A cracked hip was totally restored. The x-rays showed the crack clearly the week before and no evidence of damage the following week. The woman's surgery was canceled.

At a World Map Conference, a missionary from New Zealand called Chris from the congregation and laid hands on him to pray. Chris felt that God was calling him into the ministry and to attend Bible school. They also received prayer to have more children, as Christy was now three years old.

In the following months, Irene became pregnant with their second child. She realized how extraordinary events were coming in their lives. She remembered standing as a child in the Assembly of God Church, and recalled hearing God's gentle voice whispering to her that one day she would be a pastor's wife.

As she and Chris discussed the calling the Lord had for Chris, to attend Bible school and become a pastor, she wondered how they would be able to afford his returning to school with a growing family and no savings. One morning at 3 a.m., the Lord woke Irene and told her that Chris would be a janitor in charge of the whole school, and that they would be dorm parents. He assured her that He would supply the money for them to live. She woke up Chris to tell him what the Lord had promised her.

In a sleepy voice he responded, "Oh that's nice. You're just having one of those maternity dreams." He turned over and went back to sleep.

"No, it's not! This was no maternity dream."

The next morning, the Lord gave Irene a scripture to verify the dream:

> *Faithful is He Who is calling you [to Himself] and utterly trustworthy, and He will also do it [that is, fulfill His call by hallowing and keeping you].*

> I Thessalonians 5:24 AMP

The Philadelphia church recommended that Chris attend the Seattle Bible Training School that was affiliated with their church. So after nearly two years in their new home, recently redecorated to perfection, Chris and Irene put it up for sale and prepared to relocate to Seattle.

Not knowing where they would live or work, or how they would get the money to attend school — especially with Irene three months pregnant — they packed their meager possessions into a U-Haul truck. The Sunday before they were due to leave, they received a telephone call at the church from an apartment manager in Renton, Washington, south of Seattle, offering the position of apartment manager of a 56-unit apartment building.

Without ever seeing Chris and Irene or checking references, the man hired them over the phone. He said that God had told him to call and he was obeying what the Lord told him to do. It was another miracle.

As they closed the door to their house, Irene wondered if she would ever have her own home again. The Lord gave her the grace to look beyond the loss and to follow her husband in support of his call into the ministry.

SEATTLE

And Joshua said to the people, Sanctify yourselves [that is, separate yourselves for special holy purpose], for tomorrow the Lord will do wonders among you.

Joshua 3:5 AMP

And Naomi said, See, your sister-in-law has gone back to her people and to her god; return after your sister-in-law. And Ruth said, Urge me not to leave you, or to return from following you; for where you go, I will go; and where you lodge, I will lodge; your people shall be my people, and your God my God; Where you die, I will die, and there will I be buried. The Lord do so to me, and more also, if anything but death parts me from you.

Ruth 1:15-17 AMP

The apartment complex was located in a multicultural neighborhood, populated by Black, Hispanic, Jewish, Indian, and Oriental people. They settled into their new home, and Chris, by necessity, learned to repair heaters, electrical problems, furnaces, and the like for the 56-unit apartment building. Irene's reading was so improved that she took care of the books and finances for the apartments.

In the next months, the Lord tested them in their faith, having them deal with drunks, fire bombings, apartment dwellers bearing guns, and every other conceivable "normal" happenstance in an inner city melting pot. Chris left every morning by seven to drive 20 miles into Seattle to Bible School, sometimes wondering what new escapades would happen in his absence. Many times they wondered what they had gotten themselves into, but God spared them in every way.

One Saturday around 7 a.m., Chris and Irene woke up to the loud sound of police sirens and a huge crash as a car plummeted over a bank and into the courtyard just outside their back door. Irene maneuvered her eight-month-pregnant body out of bed and waddled behind Chris into the kitchen.

Chris ran outside, his nervous wife shouting unheeded advice behind him. Irene anxiously followed him out to meet the police.

The officers told Chris that the men in the car had escaped from the wreckage in the courtyard and were considered armed and dangerous. They asked him to accompany them to each apartment in the complex, as one of the inhabitants was probably involved with the escapees' drug operation.

Chris took off with the three police officers, running around to the other section of the complex, while Irene stood in the courtyard watching the police tow away the damaged car. She waited impatiently for about 45 minutes, fearfully wondering what had happened to Chris and the police.

As she looked around, straining to catch a glimpse of the figures scurrying in and around the apartment buildings, her attention was caught by a friend waving frantically to her from a balcony. Irene waved back, not paying much attention. But the woman kept waving and pointing to Irene's left.

She finally ignored the woman and went back into the office, frustrated that she didn't know what was going on with Chris and the police. As she went inside and pulled the screen door shut, a man ran up to the door screaming at her.

"Where's my car?" he yelled at the top of his lungs. Then he cursed at her.

"Well, I don't know," she replied, scared to death. "The police took it away." She stuttered, searching for the right thing to say, "Well, . . . I could call them. And they could get you your car. I don't have any power over the police, but maybe they would give it back to you."

The man looked at her in disbelief.

"You stupid woman!" he said. "Do you take me for a complete fool?" He put his hand on the door to open it.

"In Jesus' name get out of here!" she screamed in terror.

The man jerked back, looking in puzzlement at the pregnant woman. Then he turned and ran.

Irene reached out and pushed the door open to see if it had been locked, but the door swung freely in her hand. God had again spared her life.

Soon after, Irene went into labor with her second child. Again she had toxemia and the child came three weeks early, but the birth was much easier than her first. And so Emily was born and another of Irene's dreams had come true.

After Emily was born, Pastor Zettersten, of the Philadelphia church, stopped them on the sidewalk near the Bible school. He told them that some of the school officials had spoken with him about the need to get Chris and Irene closer to campus, to prevent the 20-mile commute and to give Irene a safer place with the children.

Would they be interested in becoming dorm parents and having Chris work as the chief custodian of the school campus? Chris and Irene looked at one another and laughed. They had thought that the apartment job was the fulfillment of Irene's "pregnancy dream," but this job offer was precisely what the Lord had told them to expect. Surely He supplied all their needs.

On a stormy cold day in February, the Taylor family moved into the dormitory in Ballard, north Seattle. The apartment was tiny, obviously converted from dormitory rooms. In the kitchen, the oven door had to be closed in order to open the refrigerator. A closet door was removed and the "room" converted into a nursery for baby Emily. In the bedroom, Irene had to crawl over her dresser to get into bed. But it was home, and it was safe — or at least safer.

Soon life returned to normal, and Irene settled into her routine of caring for the children and Chris. As she got Christy off to school one morning, she felt prompted to turn on the television while she bathed Emily in the kitchen sink.

She listened with growing interest as Phil Donahue interviewed Bruce Jenner, who spoke about his extreme difficulties in learning to read. He described how the teacher's explanation of what letters looked on the page did not match what he saw. He said that they were inverted, b's looked like d's. He could not tell his left from his right. Irene caught her breath, wrapped up the baby in a towel, and ran to the television to hear more.

He called the condition dyslexia, and he said there were several types that all stemmed from a malfunction in the connections of the brain. He told how he had learned to excel in athletics because of being humiliated by his peers who thought he was stupid because he could not learn to read. He said that he knew he wasn't stupid, but he did not learn to read until he was an adult.

Jenner went on to name other people who suffered from the condition: Cher, Albert Einstein, Abraham Lincoln.

After the show was over, Irene sat in shock. Finally it all became clear. She thanked God for showing her the interview, for giving her an explanation for her deficit in reading. She thought about how she had hung on to music as Bruce Jenner had held on to sports. She prayed and said how grateful she was that He was healing her of her embarrassing problem and allowing her to read the Bible with comprehension and understanding.

In later months, the Lord seemed to bring her attention again and again to the subject of dyslexia. A long series on the subject was on public television. At the end of the program there was a visual test. If the viewer could see elephants rather than birds, the viewer was recommended to be tested further for dyslexia.

Irene saw the elephants. Now she had criteria and definitions. And God kept confirming it so that she would have no doubt. She was introduced to the wife of a Bible school professor who taught special classes for dyslexic people. The woman further verified that Irene was dyslexic. She learned more and more about the subject, and in this knowledge she found the power and mercy to forgive those in her past who had ridiculed her in school.

The Lord gave her hints about how to maneuver around the problem. When she went shopping, she wrote the name of the store on a piece of paper before writing her check. Then she would memorize the spelling and not be embarrassed at the check-out. On being introduced to someone, she often asked for the spelling of their name, saying she wanted to get it right. In reality, she was not so much memorizing the name, but learning to spell and read. It felt so good to put a name to her condition.

In all of this, Irene had the support of her husband Chris. Each evening he would come home and she would tell him what the Lord was teaching her about dyslexia. He encouraged her and eventually she grew confident enough to enroll for classes at the Bible school. She took two years of psychology, Bible history, and five or six other subjects. She began to experience some success in school.

Irene was invited to several churches in the area to share her testimony. And now, for the first time she could read and expound upon the Word of God. And as He had promised, her understanding of the Word went far beyond her new ability to read. She was amazed and humbled by His gift. This was a great victory!

Chris continued in his own studies and matured in his faith. With the tremendous stress of full-time school, and a full-time job which required him to be on call 24 hours a day, he needed all the spiritual support he could get. The phone rang continuously. In one single day, a frustrated and irritated Irene answered 68 calls dealing with subjects such as a missing roll of toilet paper, a burned out light bulb, and a spot of dust left on a staircase.

In those whirlwind times, God began to create in Chris the heart of a servant. As he dealt patiently with the continuous demands on his time, God increased his endurance for both the work itself and the unquenchable insistence of the church fellowship. Every individual thought that their urgent need warranted Chris's immediate attention. As he handled these situations with an unfailing smile and endless patience, there emerged in him a greater understanding of people, which spilled over onto his wife and family. He was learning about the nature of love itself.

When Chris asked God why it was necessary for him to have such a heavy workload, to scrub toilets and listen to the complaints of the many people, the Lord gave him answers.

"If you will serve Me in these things, if you will submit to My Lordship, I can make you the head and not the tail," the Lord told him. "All of this is happening as part of My schooling for you. If you will submit in these small things, I will trust you with bigger things. There is no greater office than that of a servant." Obedience was the Lord's first requirement.

As Chris matured in his faith, his love for his family increased and deepened. In one of his classes the teacher assigned students to bring in a demonstration to illustrate the showing and receiving of love without using words. Chris contemplated the exercise and planned his display.

He took eight-month-old Emily to class that morning, wrapped in a blanket and wearing only a t-shirt and her diaper. When his turn came, he placed her on the table in front of the class. He took from a bag a pretty little girl slip, and a frilly green dress. Emily cooed and giggled as he carefully dressed her, putting on her tiny socks and booties. Then he combed her hair and placed his favorite little bonnet on her head. Emily rose to the occasion, smiling and laughing at her beloved daddy, waving her arms in the air.

The class was enthralled with this display of the love between a father and daughter. It was remembered for years afterward as the definitive response to the assignment.

When Emily was nine months old, Irene became pregnant again. About the same time a family from Sri Lanka moved upstairs. And again, the Lord stretched Chris and Irene, teaching them to deal with people from different cultures. The couple upstairs washed dishes at four in the morning, and Chris and Irene tried to sleep to the sound of banging pans and water running down pipes right above their heads.

There were families and young single women from Japan, Sri Lanka, Sweden, Mexico, Tanzania, Uruguay, India, Belize and other even smaller countries. They came with their cultural biases, their habits, their different ways. But they all came to study the Word of God and prepare for the ministry.

In the midst of this international atmosphere, Irene's home was like Grand Central Station. People came and went at all hours, interrupting her with Emily, waking her and Chris for the smallest "emergency." It was a fast-paced and interesting life, but one that made Irene miss the peace and quiet of her own house in Astoria. In the midst of this free-for-all, Amanda was born. And 18 months later, Melissa arrived, completing their family of four beautiful daughters.

Irene continued taking classes at the Bible college, including required courses in etiquette for pastors' wives. She was astonished at some of "rules" she was expected to follow.

She struggled through the requirements, wondering in her heart about the necessity of practicing such "good habits" as: how to be seated properly in a church pew, where to sit, acceptable and appropriate clothing for a pastor's wife, how to style her hair, and that wearing high heels makes legs look thinner and more attractive.

They discussed the fact that a pastor's wife is to be seen and not heard. A pastor's wife should only laugh in a quiet and feminine manner. The wife must support the pastor in every conceivable way, always having meals on time and being prepared at all times to have up to 10 uninvited guests for dinner.

At no time should there be a dirty dish in the pastor's kitchen sink. In an emergency, she should quickly hide the dirty dishes in the oven. The pastor's children should always have perfect manners and never be seen in dirty clothes, even during play time.

Irene wondered if she would ever achieve the level of perfection they seemed to require in a pastor's wife. As she balked, not so much at the ideas behind some of the rules, but at the fact that they were considered requirements, she took the matter to the Lord. And God told her in his gentle way that she and Chris were called to a unique ministry, and that some of these man-made rules would not apply or be necessary in their churches.

"I like you the way you are," He said. "I want you to be yourself."

And so Irene asked for discernment between what to accept and what to ignore in the many dictates she was being taught.

As Irene spooned tuna casserole onto the children's plates for the third time that week, she pondered at the differences the Lord had made in her attitudes. As a child, she had suffered through strident poverty, going for days without food. At times her family would eat that same potato soup two meals a day for as long as it took to get the next provision of government supplies. And here in the dorm there were still occasions for that potato soup.

Now, living under the influence and protection of the Holy Spirit, the food could be the same as before, but the spirit of poverty was absent from her home. She shook her head in wonder as they thankfully accepted the meager food supply still available, and were honestly happy with their lot. The difference was God. In times of plenty and in times of scarcity He supplied their needs and took away the yawning despair that accompanied the lack.

One morning, Irene and Chris stood in the kitchen looking at the totally empty cupboards and wondering if finally the Lord had forsaken them. Chris took Irene's hand and together they sat at the family table to pray. They thanked the Lord for His provision in the past and prayed specifically for their current needs.

"Lord, we need baby food, and milk, and bread. We have absolutely no food in the house." They continued praying, trying to muster the faith to continue believing in His providence.

Then Irene heard a knock at the door and went to answer it. As she opened the door, she saw a ragged, disheveled woman scurrying away from the apartment. At her feet was a large bag containing milk, bread, baby food, and every single item that they had prayed for moments before.

She called Chris, and they cried in amazement. God had truly supplied their need, even before they had prayed!

That Sunday, they met their angel of mercy, little Ida Simmons. She came to church in a coat, probably salvaged from the Civil War, and shuffled along in shoes with large holes. Her garments were old and frayed. She stuffed a hat tightly down over her uncombed hair. She looked in need of repair.

Some people in the church were nervous around Ida, thinking she was mentally ill because of her dress and the fact that she sometimes talked to herself. But she became a great friend of the Taylor family. She had a small amount of money, but she often denied herself in order to bless other people.

Irene suspected that she had a direct line to heaven. Chris and Irene would give up a need to the Lord in prayer, and within 20 minutes Ida would appear at their door with the item — the right size, the right shape, and the right color.

Socks for the children would appear in a bag on the stoop, or roller skates for Christy to take to first grade. When Chris needed to attend a church conference in Chicago to meet people in leadership roles in other churches, a path appeared that would eventually help him gain employment money.

"The Lord told me you needed this to go to Chicago," she explained, having previously known nothing of the conference.

Once, when every pair of Chris's underwear had fallen to shreds, six new pairs appeared at the door, not only in the right size, but the brand that he preferred. They had never said one word to Ida Simmons about any of these needs.

Often Chris would glance up from his labors in the school buildings to find Ida waiting patiently for his attention. He would smile and greet her, and then watch as she picked up a broom or mop and walk to the opposite end of the hall, and, working back towards him, she would help him clean the area. Other times he would go to the restrooms in a particular building, prepared to give them a healthy scrubbing, only to find a note on the door, "This bathroom is clean, Ida." She would come and clean house while Irene practiced singing for a wedding or ladies' meeting. There seemed to be no end to the ways she tried to help ease the load.

At Christmas, they tried to keep their spirits up while facing the prospect of having absolutely no gifts for their precious daughters. Doing without for themselves was one thing, but facing an empty tree for those shining faces on Christmas morning seemed more than they could bear. Again they went to the Lord for help.

On Christmas Eve, before they left to spend the holidays with Myrna and Bob, there was a tentative knock at the door. There was Ida, her arms loaded with four wrapped packages, one marked for each girl. And on Christmas morning they each unwrapped a different doll especially chosen to fit the individual personality of each girl.

Chris and Irene were overwhelmed by the love and support provided from God through this kind and generous little lady. It was as though, in His mercy, God had assigned them a personal Mother Theresa to look after them. Not only were their physical needs met, but she encouraged them to continue on and finish Bible School. Without this support they could not have gotten through this difficult time. They never forgot the generosity and kindness of this dear little woman.

As Irene continued to witness the provision of the Lord through Ida Simmons she thought back to the years of tormenting deficiency she had experienced as a child. She remembered the infrequent times her mother had asked the Lord to provide, and how He had answered those few prayers in miraculous ways. Now she could see that those years of lack need never have happened, if only her family had prayed.

For five years, the Taylor family lived in those cramped dormitory quarters. Chris got up at 5 a.m. to begin cleaning and working at the church. Then he trudged to class, sandwiching his study time between the cleaning of the five campus buildings, including the 24 bathrooms he scrubbed twice a week. His nickname in the Philadelphia church was the "Head-man."

He came home for lunch to wolf down a sandwich, and then he was gone until 4 p.m. working at the church. Irene had dinner precisely at 5 p.m., so he could eat and be out the door again by at 5:30 to study at the library. Then he returned home about 7 or 7:30 to help bathe the girls.

The arthritis in Irene's knees had worsened over the years and she was unable to kneel beside bathtub to bathe the children. So at the end of his long day Chris would kneel in the bathroom and lather the hair of his beloved daughters, scrubbing their little faces clean, then rinse them off and hand them to Irene who perched on the toilet with a dry towel. She watched him laughing and teasing with the girls and felt that she was blessed to be married to this special man. These were precious moments, the rare times the family was all together during the whirlwind days of school.

By now God had restored Irene's voice so that she was able to sing for events in the Seattle Center and for many church and secular meetings in the area. With four children and a busy husband, she still found time for her music. But her schedule helped keep her talents in perspective. It was as if God allowed her to sing, as long as she did not make music a god in her life again.

It was a time of joy and frustration, of laughter and tears, of difficulty and of healing. Their cramped quarters sometimes led to short tempers, especially in the hot summers.

But most times, the difficulties were met with humor and patience. Irene watched the children march around the apartment one day singing, "La cock-a-roach-a, la cock-a-roach-a," a song taught to them by friends visiting the dorm. She laughed and reminded them to serenade the exterminator on his weekly visits.

In her spare time, Irene counseled girls in the dorm, amazed at the problems encountered by these girls who were, for the most part, from Christian homes. Even those from "good" backgrounds had fallen victim to incest, rape, abortion, and a multitude of other evils.

Again and again the Lord reminded her that He did not necessarily remove people from the obstacles in their lives. His commitment was to walk with them through "the valley of the shadow of death." His way was to work in the midst of the trouble and repair the damage caused by those who do not choose His way. Irene began to understand that the sordid experiences of her life gave her an open door with these girls.

During the last year of Bible school, the Taylors knew the time was coming when they would leave Seattle and find their own ministry. Under the kind and capable leadership of Pastor Paul Zettersten, Chris worked as an intern pastor, preaching the first service on Sunday and leading worship. Chris deeply appreciated the example of this gracious and loving pastor, hoping that he would eventually develop similar characteristics in his own ministry. Chris and Irene did hospital visitation, and designed and organized home group meetings.

This experience helped in their eventual acceptance as pastors of the Little Church in Helena, Montana.

The move to Montana would bring many changes into their lives. Chris and Irene had never lived far from friends and family. Irene felt sharp pangs of affection for even those members of her family with whom she had experienced strong conflict. She longed to make peace with Evelyn, her sister Shirley and brother Mike. The old estrangements left from the fire and Mike's continuing incarcerations seemed like open wounds.

Once, in the middle of the night, Irene awoke to the Lord's voice: "You need to go to your grandmother."

"What, Lord?"

"If you don't go immediately to Ada, she is going to die."

"Okay, Lord," she answered sleepily.

She wakened Chris and shared with him what the Lord had said, and to her amazement, he felt a powerful confirmation in his spirit that the situation was urgent. By six o'clock she was on the bus to Newburg, Oregon.

When Irene arrived at her grandmother's house she rushed inside and found her grandfather sitting in his rocking chair and Ada standing in the kitchen in filthy clothes. Her hair was unkempt, her body unwashed. Irene stared in amazement.

"What's going on here?" she asked.

Her grandmother mumbled incoherently, shaking her head wildly.

Ernie told her that Ada had suffered a stroke and could not speak or understand when he asked her to do things. Although Ernie was quite coherent and seemed to have a solid grasp on reality, he too, appeared quite ill.

"If she's that sick, why are you asking her to do anything, Grandpa?" He looked up at her, stark fear on his face.

"She always took care of me before," he said, huge tears in his eyes.

Irene went in the kitchen and took Ada gently by the hand. She led her back into the bathroom and helped her to bathe. Then she dressed her and combed her lovely silver hair. Ada smiled at herself in the mirror and Irene's heart broke to see her beloved grandmother so helpless.

As she tidied up around the house, she noticed disturbing signs. Several guns had been taken out of their secure storage in the cabinet and were strewn around the house. There was ammunition laying around. As Irene pondered her midnight message from the Lord, she realized that things were much worse than she had expected.

Irene got the house in order and fixed a nice meal. And that evening they sat around the kitchen table, talking and then singing the old hymns together. Irene and Ernie laughed and enjoyed themselves immensely, and Ada laughed too. But her frustration with her physical limitations was evident.

Irene talked with her grandparents about Jesus.

"When people get to the end of their lives," she said, "He is the only thing they have to hold onto."

Ernie asked her to sing "Precious Lord, Take My Hand," and she sang for them. Then she reminded them how important it is to know, beyond the shadow of a doubt, that the next step a person takes beyond life will take place in heaven. Her grandfather agreed with her.

And so they all retired.

At five the next morning, Ada woke Irene from a sound sleep, "speaking" to her frantically. Irene struggled to understand what

Ada was trying to tell her.

"Nnni nannnth nuuu nnnnis."

"You can't what, Grandma?"

"Nnnnuu nnnis."

"You can't do this," Irene said. Ada nodded vehemently.

"You help me, right?" Ada continued. Irene understood her more clearly.

"You help me, right?!"

"Sure, I'll help you, Grandma," she said, thinking that Ada wanted help with the house or something. Then Ernie appeared at the door.

"Ada, come on," he said, "You need to go back to bed and let Irene rest." Ada looked back at Irene, pleading for help.

In the morning Irene rose early, planning to see what arrangements could be made to care for Ada. She called the doctors to get more information about Ada's physical and mental condition, and was given advice on places to contact about home health care.

Before any plan could be formulated, she went to help Ada get up and dress only to find her loading a .22 rifle in her bedroom. She struggled with her grandmother to get the gun away. Irene was astounded at the strength of the wiry little woman. They broke out of the house and fought on the front lawn.

Irene was at the end of her rope. "In the name of Jesus," she shouted, "let go of this gun." She gave a mighty tug and the rifle flew out of Ada's hands. They both fell down in the grass, exhausted from their efforts.

Then Ada struggled to her feet, and ran back into the house. Irene jumped up in alarm and followed her finding her, only to find her in the kitchen struggling with Ernie over a butcher knife.

"Put that down!" he shouted at her.

Suddenly all the fight went out of her. Ada slumped into a chair at the table and sobbed uncontrollably, pounding her head against her hands on the table. Irene called for an ambulance. The next day, Ada was placed in a nursing home. Irene called her uncle to come and care for Ernie. Boarding the bus back to Seattle, Irene felt weary yet thankful to God for His intervention.

Chris and Irene returned to Astoria the following weekend to say their last good-byes. As they drove away, Irene's heart was heavy with fear for her grandparents. Would the other grandchildren check on them to make sure they were properly cared for? Who would be there to answer the Lord's call and run to their assistance in the next emergency? With a burdened heart she rode with Chris to Montana.

LITTLE CHURCH

*All the commandments which I command you this day you shall
be watchful to do, that you may live, and multiply, and go in and
possess the land which the Lord swore to give to your fathers. And
you shall (earnestly) remember all the way which the Lord your God
led you these forty years in the wilderness, to humble you, and to prove
you, to know what was in your [mind and] heart, whether you would
keep His commandments or not. And He humbled you and allowed
you to hunger, and fed you with manna, which you did not know;
that He might make you recognize and personally know that man
does not live by bread only, but man lives by every word that pro-
ceeds out of the mouth of the Lord. Your clothing did not become old
upon you, nor did your foot swell, these forty years. Know also in your
[mind and] heart that, as a man disciplines and instructs his son,
so the Lord your God disciplines and instructs you. So you shall keep
the commandments of the Lord your God, to walk in His ways and
(reverently) fear Him. For the Lord your God is bringing you into a
good land, a land of brooks of water, of fountains and springs, flowing forth in valleys and hills; A land of wheat and barley, and vines
and fig trees and pomegranates, a land of olive trees and honey, A
land in which you shall eat food without shortage, and lack nothing
in it, a land whose stones are iron, and out of whose hills you can
dig copper. When you have eaten and are full, then you shall bless
the Lord your God for all the good land which He has given you.*

Deuteronomy 8:1-10 AMP

Irene began to meet people in Montana who did not know her background or history. In a way it was refreshing to live apart from the familial prejudice that had colored her reputation in the small Oregon-Washington communities of her childhood. But now her character stood on its own.

And the reality was — though God had delivered her from the brokenness of her family and given her a husband who loved and cherished her, and though He had begun a work of healing that was far from finished — she still retained some negative personality traits from her childhood experiences.

The arrogant spirit that she had felt on the day she took the broom from her mother was far from bridled. The childish anger and resentment birthed by the cruelty she had known from infancy had left her as a person who had to be in control at all times. She had a difficult time balancing the need to have her own way with the gracious and merciful methods of the Lord.

Even in the making of the decision to move to Montana, Irene had pushed and maneuvered Chris into the decision. Although her faith in God was strong, she experienced a powerful impatience to leave the dorm and return to "normal" life, to have a home of her own, to regain the personal space and privacy that they had relinquished living in the dorm. Her desire to control caused much difficulty in becoming a "successful" pastor's wife.

Chris, exhausted from his hours of labor as a janitor and student, had fallen into some negative habits of his own. He relied on Irene to "fix" a variety of situations, including his habitual tardiness and forgetfulness about appointments. He hated talking on the phone and was perfectly satisfied to lay this type of chore off on his capable wife. But as he handed over various duties to Irene, this enhanced her reputation as the "boss."

Chris tended to be quiet and polite in public, but had a powerful temper which raged out of control at home. When Irene and the children knew he was angry, they quickly scattered until the storm blew over.

With these imbalances firmly in place, they took over as pastors of Little Church.

The church sat on a foothill right under Mount Helena in Helena, Montana, the capital city. There were about 20 members in the congregation which was some 30 years old. It had been established by a female pastor, Monida Vaughn, an unusual occurrence even for an independent church.

Miss Vaughn had died only 18 months before their arrival in Montana, and in that time, with the exception of a brief stay by one pastor, the church had floundered without leadership. The membership was very opinionated and operated within stringent rules set down by the church board members under the powerful influence of their former female pastor.

Flowers were placed under her picture which was hung in a prominent position in the church foyer. The pictures of 10 other deceased members lined another wall. In the sanctuary, an arrangement of plastic flowers had been saved from Monida Vaughn's grave and placed in a position of importance near the pulpit. These powerful reminders of the dead gave the church the impression of a funeral home.

Chris and Irene tried to ease into the pastorate without making too many waves. But as time passed, they butted heads with church leadership with increasing intensity, trying to bring appropriate order to the church and to invite the Holy Spirit into the position of leadership.

After a few weeks a neighbor, not a member of the church, told them about the first pastor who had come after the death of Monida Vaughn.

"They locked him out of his office one day and said you can't come back in the church," he told them. "You're squandering money and preaching heresy. All the guy had said was that they should let go of Monida Vaughn and that by their actions they could kill the church. But they just packed up his belongings and told him to leave, just like that. I pray that the same thing doesn't happen to you."

"It will be hard," Chris responded, "but I think we can weather the storm. After all, the church is growing by the day."

They worked on church music and kicked off a new Sunday school program. Soon the situation seemed to calm down, although periodically the old rules would seem to jump up and hit them in the face.

Irene and the children were not allowed in the kitchen of the church building. In Sunday school, if one of the children got the slightest bit of crayon on a table there would be a huge uproar.

Baptisms were not allowed in the church baptismal because the church leadership did not want water to get on their polished wooden floors and carpet.

One evening after a church meeting Irene was cornered by a riotous group of church women who demanded that the pictures of the deceased members hanging in the foyer be moved into the sanctuary, behind the pulpit. Irene was flabbergasted by the whole idea but struggled to hold her temper.

"You need to speak to Chris about this," she answered, knowing that he would not stand for this.

"But you can make him do it," they said.

"I will not make him do anything. It is not my place. You go talk to Chris," she continued and fled from the mob.

They proceeded to corner Chris who suggested that the matter be brought before the board.

"I do not think it is appropriate to have those pictures in the sanctuary," he said, saving his anger for an explosion with Irene when he got home. And so the pictures stayed where they were, in the foyer.

On the anniversary of Monida Vaughn's death, one of the women asked for permission to speak to the congregation in memory of the sacrifices Monida had made for them to build this wonderful church. Chris thought it over and could see no real harm in honoring the memory of the woman who was responsible for starting the church and donating most of the funds for the building and grounds.

But when the time came for the woman and her friends to speak, they orated for over 10 minutes about their precious Monida Vaughn, and then led an extensive prayer for the spirit of the dead woman. Chris and Irene were appalled.

During these first months of difficulty at Little Church, Irene tried to keep contact with her grandparents. Eventually Grandpa Ernie grew sicker and died, leaving Ada alone in the nursing home. An uncle called to tell Irene that her grandmother was not doing well in the nursing home, and after much prayerful consideration, Chris and Irene decided to bring Ada back to Montana with them.

When they called Ada, she asked them to come and take her to Montana to be near them, because none of the family visited her or took care of her needs. Even though Irene knew that this would put a wedge between herself and her family, she flew to Newburg and brought Ada home with her under a shadow of their disapproval. When her grandmother called her to come and take her out of the nursing home, she knew it was the Lord's will. She loaded her grandmother and the three small boxes that contained all her worldly possessions onto the plane and headed east.

In Montana they found a clean and competent nursing home that was close to town, so the family could visit her regularly and care for her.

Even though the pastor and the church leadership were at powerful odds over so many issues, the membership decided to build the Taylor family a new house on the church property. Irene was ecstatic, but doubtful about both the motives and the outcome of this new adventure.

They designed the house with a huge basement, perfect for indoor roller skating, and with an extra bedroom and bath. The upstairs had four bedrooms and two bathrooms. Irene planned for the use of their new 4200 square foot space with dreams of having her own room for sewing, crafts, and laundry upstairs. Christy, as the oldest, would have her own room downstairs.

Then, at the last minute the committee, without consulting the pastor, changed the floor plans, eliminating the laundry room upstairs and making other modifications. They informed the Taylors that the basement of the house would be considered off limits for the use of the family.

When Chris asked why these changes were being made, he was told, "We know you guys lived in a dorm before. Don't you think this is a lot better? Why should you complain about anything that we do." Again Chris and Irene sat in amazement.

Two months later Chris moved the last of their meager belongings into their beautiful new home while Irene stood outside studying the photograph of Monida Vaughn which hung ominously over her new front door.

The church leadership maintained "ownership" of the property through many less than subtle practices. They entered the house at will, never knocking. Several times, in fury, she would be taking a shower, and would have to cover herself and peek out to see who was invading her privacy. At least in the dorm people had bothered to knock. Every member of the council had a key to the house, so the lock was no deterrent to this invasion.

About this time, 14 pastors in Helena, including Chris, joined in a concerted effort against the growth of cult movements which had taken root in the community. Chris informed the church leadership of his activities with these other Christian men, and the council indicated that they supported his efforts. But as some members of the church had close family or friends involved with the various cult movements, Chris suspected that they were not altogether united in their enthusiasm about this outreach. He felt an underlying current of criticism about his stand.

On another occasion, Chris was accused of taking 10 dollars from the offering plate. Chris demanded to know the details of the accusation. The board members hemmed and hawed around and finally someone said that a witness had seen a 10 dollar bill in the offering plate, and that later the bill was missing. Chris stood with his mouth hanging open.

"You must be joking," he said in amazement. "Tell me what is really going on here."

They refused to name the witness or be more specific about the incident.

In exasperation, Chris simply expounded upon the biblical standards for accusation against an elder, rebuking them sharply and leaving.

In the midst of constant agitation, the church grew from the original 20 people to a membership of over 50 adults and their children. It was a powerful ministry, with many people receiving the Lord Jesus as their Savior. It may have been this sudden growth which eventuated the circumstances that ended Chris and Irene's pastorate at Little Church.

Church policy designated that new members must declare membership a full year before they were allowed to vote on matters before the congregation. And so briefly before the influx of new members were eligible to vote, the old guard called a board meeting.

"You are bringing too many new people into the congregation. We will lose control of the finances of the church," one member said. "We don't want all these new people involved in our church."

"They will take our money," another added.

And so Chris and Irene were voted out of the pastorate, by 12 people, without being allowed to say a proper good-bye to their many friends within the church body.

In spite of the many problems, it had been a fruitful ministry. People had been brought closer to Jesus and the church had grown. One young man dedicated his life to the ministry, going on to attend Seattle Bible College, Chris' alma mater.

The newer members were devastated at the Taylors' removal from Little Church. No explanation was offered for the disappearance of the pastor and his family, and in the following weeks, many of them approached Chris and Irene for some accounting for the board's action. They remained as puzzled as Chris and Irene.

Chris and Irene had a taste of pastoral ministry, but now with it torn from them, their future seemed uncertain at best. In their sorrowful prayers that evening the Lord gave Chris and Irene a scripture:

> *Day and night they go about on its walls; iniquity and mischief are in its midst. Violence and ruin are within it; fraud and guile do not depart from its streets and market place. For it is not an enemy who reproaches and taunts me; then I might bear it; nor one who has hated me who insolently vaunts himself against me; then I might hide from him. But it was you, a man my equal, my companion and my familiar friend; We had sweet fellowship together, and used to walk to the house of God in company. Let desolations and death come suddenly upon them; let them go down alive to Sheol [the place of the dead]; for evils are in their habitations, in their hearts and their inmost part . . . He has redeemed my life in peace from the battle that was against me [so that none came near me], for they were many who strove with me.*

> Psalm 55:10-15, 18 AMP

And the next morning, He gave them another scripture:

It is better to dwell in a corner of the housetop [on a flat oriental roof, exposed to all kinds of weather] than in a house shared with a nagging, quarrelsome and faultfinding woman.

Proverbs 21:9 AMP

HELENA

God is not a man, that He should lie, nor a son of man, that he should change His mind. Does He speak and then not act? Does He promise and not fulfill? I have received a command to bless; He has blessed, and I cannot change it.

Numbers 23:19,20 KJV

But who can endure the day of His coming? Who can stand when He appears? For He will be like a refiner's fire or a launderer's soap. He will sit as a refiner and purifier of silver; He will purify the Levites and refine them like gold and silver. Then the Lord will have men who will bring offerings in righteousness, and the offerings of Judah and Jerusalem will be acceptable to the Lord as in days gone by, as in former years.

Malachi 3:2-4 NIV

Have mercy on me and be gracious to me, O Lord, for I am weak (faint and withered away). O Lord, heal me, for my bones are troubled.

Psalm 6:2 AMP

The firing of a pastor ignites the grapevine telegraph system, and by noon the next day, the news was all over town. The Taylors received many phone calls of support from other Christians in the community, calls received in a fog of shock. The only thing that was crystal clear was that they needed a place to stay.

A neighbor appeared at the door and offered them the use of his finished basement that had a bath.

Teach Me How You Walked

Lord teach me how You walked.
This earth is a hard place to live.
I am so glad You came
And showed us the way.

I know You felt pain
When people hated You,
And You feel my pain now
When no one else can.
Lord, teach me how You walked.

When You had no place to lay Your head,
When people said so many bad things
To You and about You,
Just lies.
Lord, teach me how You walked

When people took everything from You
And beat you and spat on You.
Then they nailed You to the cross.
How could You do that for me?
Lord, teach me how You walked.

Lord, I have given all that I have.
I have given my life,
My home and friends and my family's love.
I feel so much pain in my heart.
I have nothing left and no place to go.
Lord, teach me how You walked.

Please Lord, heal this pain I have in my life.
Don't just leave me in this desert.
How can I go on under this load.
Help me to be stronger when problems come.
Lord, teach me how You walked.

Irene Taylor

In a short time, the family gratefully moved their possessions into these cramped quarters, storing the excess in the garage.

As the first evening came and went, Chris maintained a facade in front of the children, pretending that he knew everything would work out, but feeling the immeasurable weight of the failure of his first pastorate. Irene busied herself caring for the children, ages two to eight, and wondered secretly if they would ever be pastors again.

As she tucked Christy into her sleeping bag on the basement floor, Christy caught her mother by the arm.

"Jesus hasn't forgotten us, Mommy. This is just like a picture. We can only see the beginning, but he has the brush strokes all planned to make a beautiful painting."

Irene kissed her daughter gently and turned away, hiding her flowing tears.

> *Though the fig tree does not blossom, and there be no fruit on the vines; [though] the product of the olive fail, and the fields yield no food; though the flock be cut off from the fold, and there be no cattle in the stalls; Yet I will rejoice in the Lord, I will exult in the [victorious] God of my salvation! The Lord God is my strength, my personal bravery and my invincible army; He makes my feet like hinds' feet, and will make me to walk [not to stand still in terror, but to walk] and make [spiritual] progress upon my high places [of trouble, suffering or responsibility]!*

> Habakkuk 3:17-19 AMP

For the next five weeks, Chris pounded the pavement around Helena, searching for employment and more permanent housing for his family. Some days he found temporary labor and brought home a few dollars to buy potatoes for soup or beans to feed them. In the evening he poured over the scriptures, scrutinizing them for some explanation, some reason for all of these devastating events. The Lord showed him many scriptures to sustain him, such as:

> *If you have raced with me on foot and they have worn you out, how can you compete with horses? If you*

stumble in safe country, how will you manage in the thickets by the Jordan? Your brothers, your own family — they have betrayed you; they have raised a loud cry against you. Do not trust them, though they speak well of you. I will forsake my house, abandon my inheritance; I will give the one I love into the hands of her enemies. My inheritance has become to me like a lion in the forest. She roars at me; therefore I hate her. Has not my inheritance become to me like a speckled bird of prey that other birds of prey surround and attack? Go and gather all the wild beasts; bring them to devour. Many shepherds will ruin my vineyard and trample down my field; they will turn my pleasant field into a desolate wasteland. It will be made a wasteland, parched and desolate before me; the whole land will be laid waste because there is no one who cares.

Jeremiah 12:5-11 AMP

They lived on beans and potato soup, the staples of Irene's childhood. At first Irene could not force herself to choke down the meager foodstuffs, asking God why they had been reduced to this state again. The kids loved them. But Irene gagged at the thought of the nightly pot of legumes.

After a short time the Lord spoke to her, "It's okay to eat beans when you love Jesus."

"What do you mean, Lord? This is how I lived as a child. Surely your children don't live in the same poverty I grew up in," she questioned.

"Irene, beans are good, healthy food. It's not the lack of food that you experienced as a child that has so bruised you. In your childhood there was great disorder and cruelty. Those were the truly damaging events. But when you have your trust in Me even eating beans isn't bad."

And so Irene ate the bowl of beans.

Better is a dinner of herbs where love is, than a stalled ox and hatred therewith.

Proverbs 15:17 KJV

And so Chris and Irene stayed in the wasteland for a short time. There, without material possessions, and having no friends or family on which they could lean, God began a deep healing and ministry within each of them. It was a time of serious reflection and questioning of their commitment to the ministry.

It was clear that God did not have an easy way planned for them, and that their ministry had to be based entirely on faith in God. If they could learn that God was and always would be their only source for everything, they would clearly see Him bless and keep them.

As the weeks and months went by, they got a place to live in the HUD housing complex for 52 dollars a month. And as they subsisted on potato soup and beans, even the children came to see that day by day Almighty God met their needs.

Twice a week they visited Grandma Ada at the nursing home, and periodically they brought her home with them to share a meager meal and fellowship together. In these sparse surroundings the love of their family prospered and grew.

For a whole year, Chris found no permanent work. At that time in Montana things seemed worse than during the depression. People waited two and three hours for a chance at a minimum wage job. Once Chris stood in line for a whole day trying to get a job frying hamburgers at McDonald's, only to be denied because of his education. And so, with little food and nowhere else to go, they prayed and asked God what to do.

And yet, as God had promised, their basic needs were met. Total strangers came to their door bearing boxes of deer meat or other groceries. Several times, they came out of church to find the back of their car filled with canned goods.

They learned to read the Bible together as a family, and it sustained them. They learned to pray together, sometimes with the children leading, asking God to supply their needs.

Even the most mundane necessity was brought before the Lord. Four-year-old Amanda prayed one evening for a pair of red pants to replace the ragged ones she wore to play in every day.

"Dear Jesus," she prayed. "I need some red pants. You are the only one I can ask, because Mommy and Daddy don't have any money, but you have lots of money. Could I have some red pants, please?" Within a week, three pairs of red pants came in the mail.

Irene found two more pairs in the basement. Amanda now had five pairs of red pants.

In these troubled times Chris and Irene drew together as never before. As time passed, Chris' temper mellowed and he became more tolerant of the weaknesses and foibles of those around him. He learned maturity in dealing with people and learned how to be the head of his family without manipulating them to maintain control. His quiet strength became the center-post of vitality to which the family came for guidance.

Irene also matured. She learned that it was not necessary for her to maintain an iron control of the situation when Jesus was invited to be Lord. She gradually learned to loosen her grasp on her children and her husband, and not to demand her way in every instance.

She asked the Lord specifically what to pray for Chris, what he needed the most, and the Lord taught her a lesson about praying and not "saying."

"When I give you a problem, Irene," He told her, "I want you to pray about it, not talk about it. Pray, not say."

"What do you mean, Lord?" she asked.

"When you pray, you're not controlling anybody. If you're praying for them, you're just letting God use that outcome." He said, "I want you to pray that Chris will be more decisive and directive. It is a constant prayer you need to pray for your husband."

Two days after he told Irene what to pray, Chris said that the Lord was really showing him that he needed to be more decisive and directive in what he did. Irene thanked the Lord once again and acknowledged that He knew exactly what He was doing in their lives.

In this way, Irene learned to release people into the restoring power of the Lord. And the Lord showed her that her desire to "fix" people and situations had its roots in her desire to control them, roots in Irene's remaining sense of insecurity. As she turned this insecurity over to the Lord, He began new sets of lessons and prescriptions to bring her into wholeness.

At church she tried not to remind Chris about things, taking her hand away from his life and letting God be God. And as she relinquished control, God began to create the kind of man that He wanted for His work, and the perfect husband for Irene. She still told him her thoughts and opinions, but then left the situation completely up to him, sink or swim. And the Lord grew Chris in wisdom.

These lessons were long in the learning and not easy. But as the Lord was invited to be the potter, and the whole Taylor family learned to act as the clay, peace and joy reigned as they learned to accept His Lordship, to totally believe that "all things work together for good, to them who love God and are called according to His purpose" (Romans 8:28 NIV).

By now they had moved Grandma Ada into a nursing home just outside East Helena. Irene continued her twice-a-week visits, often taking the children to see their great- grandmother. And as she drove the back gravel road to the nursing home, she often pondered about the difficulties of their situation. At times she wondered if they were truly walking in the will of God. Was He with them? Did Jesus still care?

The road meandered through the hilly country, past a cement relay station where huge trucks came to deliver mountainous boulders to crush in the thundering machine. At the station, the trucks delivered their heavy burden and pulled around the other side to be loaded with gravel. The enormous trucks rolled endlessly up the road on tires taller than a man.

Irene drove, blissfully unaware of the heavy trucks using the road, talking to Melissa and listening to her little girl stories. Suddenly a loud voice yelled at her to stop.

Startled at the sound, she said aloud, "Why should I stop? I'm not going too fast. Melissa's in her seatbelt. Everything's fine."

"Stop," the voice insisted.

Melissa looked curiously at her mother. Irene wondered if she also heard the voice.

"Why? Why should I stop? Did you hear that, Melissa?" she asked, wondering if she was hearing things.

"Hear what, Mommy?"

"Stop now, or you'll die," the voice said.

This time Irene did not hesitate. As she put on the brakes and pulled to the side of the road, a tremendous truck, loaded to the limit with a colossal weight of freshly crushed gravel, careened by them, missing the car by inches. The car shook as the mighty weight lurched down the road. The driver, from his high angle, never saw Irene's car and continued speedily on his way.

Irene sat for a moment, willing herself to breathe. And then she realized, perhaps for the first time, that God would not directly intervene to save her and the life of her youngest daughter if He did not have a purpose in keeping them alive.

"I'm sure glad I listened to Jesus, sweetie," she said shakily to her young daughter.

"Yeah, Mom," Melissa answered. "It would be fun to go to heaven with you. But not today, okay?"

Irene threw back her head and laughed with heartfelt thankfulness and joy.

Chris and Irene became active in a penitentiary ministry, making numerous trips to Deerlodge Prison under the auspices of the East Helena Foursquare Church. Chris would find day labor for a few days, then load up the car and drive 50 miles to the isolated little town which housed the state prison. There they ministered to 40 or 50 men who gathered with them each Friday night to sing and praise the Lord. The relationships Chris and Irene formed with the prisoners gave them a new perspective on the purpose of ministry.

Within those high prison walls, they experienced enormous freedom in worship. Every Friday night they approached the facility with joy and anticipation of the masterful way God moved in the prisoners' lives. Within this institution they experienced total acceptance and affection. And as their relationships deepened with trust and friendship, many of the inmates gave their hearts to Christ, experiencing the healing power of forgiveness, and the strengthening of a healthy sense of self-esteem.

Chris preached a hard word to these men that reached through the tough armor they wore around their hearts. He talked about how they conned themselves, and God, and other people. He spoke about how that con can become the very center of your life, to could cover up how you really feel. And then he spoke about how the presence of God can give you freedom, even in prison. At the end of the service they would all stand and sing. And during their ministry many of these troubled people accepted the Lord Jesus as their Savior and Lord.

Most of the prisoners were very young and the stories of their backgrounds reflected cycles of the powerful bondage of alcoholism, drug abuse, and family dysfunction. One man was 37 years old, and his 19-year-old son was also a prisoner. They came to the Christian meetings because they were not allowed to speak together any other time during the week. Eventually they both came to know the Lord.

Another prisoner, one of the main suppliers of drugs inside Montana State Prison, accepted the Lord and dumped $5,000 to $6,000 worth of drugs down the toilet in his cell. As the prison grapevine spread the word of his salvation, a contract was put out on his life and he had to be transferred to another prison. But he was saved and filled with the Holy Spirit and another life was changed.

No matter what they thought of themselves, God showed Chris and Irene that as they received Jesus in their lives and received His forgiving grace, He could make them feel good about themselves. Murderers, drug addicts, rapists, men guilty of every conceivable sin, came to know redemption as they made peace with Almighty God.

The second year away from Little Church found the Taylors drawn back into the ministry. They were voted onto the staff of East Helena Foursquare Family Life Center and served there as co-pastors. Irene worked on the counseling staff. Within the support of this group of dedicated Christians, they got their feet back on the ground in the ministry.

It was a unique time in their lives, requiring a certain special grace to live as pastor and to share pastoral authority.

God taught Chris that even a well-meaning pastor can make the ministry an idol in his life. A man of God must keep his priorities in line, and follow the Holy Spirit. The Lord reminded Chris that his own family should sometimes take precedence over his church family.

In June the family took a brief trip to Astoria, to check on their house and prepare it for new renters. Ada was now happily settled in the nursing home in Montana, perfectly content with regular visits from Chris, Irene and the children. But Irene was aware, as they returned to Oregon, that her family was still upset that Ada had been "taken" from them.

Irene called Evelyn several times during their short trip, but she never seemed to be at home. Then one morning, as she and her friend Jan walked downtown to do some shopping, she saw her mother stumbling out of the Brass Rail Tavern.

Irene ran over to her mother and hugged her, but Evelyn remained stiff as a board. Irene stepped back to tell Evelyn how glad she was to see her, Evelyn started shouting vile and obscene words to her daughter.

She cursed Irene, and she cursed her grandchildren. She shouted that Irene's children would never grow up to have a place to live or amount to anything, that they would rise up to hate Irene. Jan drew back from the verbal onslaught and people on the street stared at the violent scene.

Evelyn continued, shaking her finger in Irene's face, "When Chris leaves you and you have no place to go, you'll understand what I'm talking about. Then your kids will need a place and they'll have to come to see me, won't they? But I won't lift a finger to help you. You took my mother away from me, and you will pay for it." Tears of shame and sorrow washed down Irene's face.

"You've always been ashamed that I'm your mother. You've never liked me or cared for what I did. You've always been wrapped up in your own feelings and your own things," Evelyn screamed at her weeping daughter.

Irene's heart broke as she listened to her mother's accusations. She prayed desperately, "Oh Lord, what can I say to her? Please Jesus, help me."

Eventually Evelyn ran out of angry words, and in that tense and quiet moment the Lord told Irene what to say.

With tears still running down her cheeks she said, "Momma, I thank God that you're my mother. I love you, and I care about you. I know that it hurt when Grandma came to Montana, but I thought I was doing the right thing for you and the family. If the day ever comes that you don't have a place to go or a place to live, or you think no one cares about you, I will do the same for you, Momma. You can come and live at my house and I will help you. I want you to know that I care about you too."

And she hugged Evelyn, still stiff and unyielding, and said, "I wouldn't ever want any other mom but you, because God gave you as my mother."

Evelyn glared daggers at Irene and said, "I don't believe you."

That hurt more than anything.

Then as Evelyn turned and stumbled back into the tavern, Jan wrapped her arms around her sobbing friend and held on tight.

"Don't hold this against her, Irene," she said. "Just forgive her."

"I'll try, Jan," she answered.

Later in the afternoon, as Irene stood in the shower wishing that the water could wash the hurt away, the Lord spoke to her: "When your mother is old, she will know Me — and you will have a friendship with her that will last forever."

His words warmed her heart. She repeated them over and over to herself, and in this special assurance, the hurts were soothed and healed.

Soon after they returned to Montana, Irene's knees, still suffering from the recurring effects of juvenile arthritis, became intolerably painful. When the church invited an evangelist named Dick Joyce to speak, she planned to go up front and ask him to pray for her. Not only was she suffering from the pain in her knees, but she still felt somewhat disjointed from losing her home and still not having a sense of belonging.

At the meeting, Dick Joyce laid his hands on her knees and began to pray for her in a powerful way. And as he finished he said, "God's going to help you with fear and just break that out of your life, so you won't be afraid anymore."

Irene was amazed. It was as if he had read her mind as she sorted through the myriad of powerful fears that held her in bondage. Then suddenly she was on the floor. She could hear the people around her, in a vague way, but she no longer cared about what they were doing. She laid there feeling as if her head rested in someone's lap, sensing their fingers stroking her hair and saying, "It's all right; you're okay."

She felt as though the Lord was sitting there. He took her hand, and they were in another place.

"You remember the place where I took you when your brother and your nephew died in the fire, Irene?" He asked. "Now you are spiritually sound that I can show you more, so you won't be afraid anymore about life. Let Me take your hand, and I'll meet you at that place."

As Irene saw the picture in her mind of where she and Jesus had walked with Sammy and David, she found herself walking again on the roadway.

Then Jesus was there, and He talked again about Sammy and David and said, "Now remember, it was not your fault."

But even as an adult, she still struggled with her guilt over their deaths. The remorse and torment still haunted her like a nightmare.

He looked at her gently and said, "Let's go past that. I want you to look around and look at the trees and grass and smell things. Keep your eyes open, and see what this is like."

"Why, Lord?" she asked. But He did not answer.

"Just smell the clean fresh air," He said.

She took a deep breath.

The grass was a beautiful, shimmering green, as if the color itself was alive. The wind would hit the trees, flipping the leaves up to reveal their golden underside and producing a soft twinkling music that rode along the gentle breeze. A river cascaded down over the little hill, its glistening water leaping from the surfaces of multi-colored stones shining like gems from the treasure chest of a giant.

"Now look under your feet."

Irene chuckled as the transparent gold pavement reminded her of the yellow brick road in the "Wizard of Oz." But this was real gold.

And He said, "I've only let you see this because of the hard things that you have gone through in your life. I want to teach you to look for the beautiful things around you. I want you to learn to not focus on the pain, but to look for the treasures that I put in your life every day. I do not want you to miss these small things that I use to lift your spirits. Now I am going to take your hand, and you're going to walk with Me on this street and see some of the wonders of your home in heaven."

He took her hand, and they walked into the kingdom.

"I'm so glad that you're My daughter and that I'm your father. I will always take care of you, Irene. I want you to stop worrying about never having a place or feeling like you belong," He said.

"But Lord, so many times I do feel that way."

He took her hand, and they walked. On both sides, fields of thick flowers lined their way, filling the air with their perfume.

As they approached the crest of the hill, shimmering heat seemed to rise off the road. A vertical rainbow of iridescent colors quivered up from the golden bricks. In the distance, Irene could see the city itself, solid gold with luminous violet, blue, orange, yellow, and purple, like a prism shining up into the brilliant sky. The light was so bright it hurt her eyes. In the distance Irene could see the city of heaven, where God dwells.

As they walked down the hillside, suddenly they were standing at an enormous gate. Its pearl-like surface, brilliant white with iridescent pink, gold, and blue extended both wider and higher than the eye could see. Irene gasped at its beauty, reaching out to run her fingers over the textured surface. As she realized that the surface was the gate itself, she looked in vain for a handle or a knocker.

Jesus turned to her, smiling at her astonishment, and said, "Daughter, this door is never closed to you. It will always be open."

As He touched the door, the whole gate folded back like a curtain. He took her hand like a gallant gentleman inviting an honored guest to enter the court of the King. He said, "Come in," and together they walked inside.

Irene's heart filled with tears of humility. With this simple gesture, Almighty God, Father of the Universe, Savior of the World, Creator of all things, put her in a place of honor that she could never hope to earn or deserve. By His righteousness, she was made worthy of this position. He truly loved her as His own personal and beloved daughter and friend. This show of love was beyond her comprehension.

Then He looked at her, took both hands in His and said, "Maybe you will never feel like you have a home or a place on earth, but remember daughter, know and never forget that you have a home with Me, and I'm waiting for you. You don't have to worry about not having a place of your own.

"When hard times come and you think about the difficulties in your life, or when you feel disjointed and you want to come home and visit me, your Dad, here in heaven, all you have to do is think about this time that I took you to the door. All you have to do is say, 'Let me in; I want to come home.' I'll open that gate and I'll be right there with you in that special place that only you and I know about.

"I create a special place for each one of my children that is unique to that specific child. And here is where you will meet Me."

They walked into the courtyard. The same strange and beautiful music created by the wind in the trees played more loudly here, its haunting melodies quieting the spirit and washing over her in waves of joy. The courtyard was bordered by huge white pillars supporting an immense circular balcony planted all round with unbelievable flowers, trees, and vines. Off the courtyard, both above and below the balcony, were dozens of tiny rooms. The floor was crystal clear like one enormous diamond.

In the center of the massive room, a fountain gushed up out of the floor itself. The water spouted high into the air, then rushed in effervescent splendor back down into itself, forming tiny glittering prisms of colored light as it returned to its source. Music seemed to emanate from every surface — the trees, the plants, the water. The air smelled so pure and clean, colored with the fragrance of a million radiant roses.

And Jesus took her hand and asked, "Will you dance with Me in My courtyard?"

Irene was suddenly conscious of her crooked and clumsy legs, swelled with arthritis. The thought of her awkward movements filled her with painful embarrassment.

"Me, dance with You, Father? How can I dance with You? You know I feel so clumsy. I can't dance." Her face burned with humiliation.

But Jesus said, "Take My hand, and I'll show you."

As she reached for His hand, she looked into His face — and in His smile the pain and shame subsided. They danced round and round in the courtyard, laughing, her feet and legs flying in graceful movements with the heavenly music. He began to sing to her, sweet music that lifted her heart. Time stood still as they danced and danced.

After a time they stopped and He said, "Are you sure now that you are okay? And that you can dance?"

She laughed softly and nodded.

"I'll save you a dance when you come back to be home with Me forever. Now you understand and know that you always have a place with Me. You are My special darling. And nobody, nobody in the whole universe from the beginning of time to the end of time will be My special daughter as you are, because there is nobody else like you. You're My one and only. My one and only."

Then Irene was settled gently back in her body. Her head still rested in someone's lap. The pain was gone from her knees. She got up and began to share her experience with the people in the church and found that others had experienced similar visitations from the Lord.

She shared this vision of the Lord showing her His desire to have a special relationship with each one of His children — that every child of God is unique and important to Him, and that He desires close fellowship in that secret place with each and every one of us. There, hidden in His tabernacle, we can find release and renewal in that special relationship we have with Him.

> *One thing I have desired of the Lord, that will I seek after; that I may dwell in the house of the Lord all the days of my life, to behold the beauty of the Lord, and to inquire in His temple. For in the time of trouble He shall hide me in His pavilion: in the secret of His tabernacle shall He hide me; He shall set me up upon a rock.*
>
> Psalm 27:4-5 KJV

The Lord had given Irene a vision of heaven, a picture of a special place, hidden so that the enemy could not approach her. He had given her a resting place where she could not be hurt, but always accepted and reassured, a place where she could feel the unconditional love and approval of the Lord.

In future times, the Lord would gently remind her, "When you feel out of place or are sinking into depression, Irene, come back to that place. Let Me say those words to you again, to refresh your spirit."

Or He would tell her: "If you wander away from My presence or get too far away from My guidance, I will draw you back to the memory of that courtyard, to the memory of the dance."

This statement from the Lord Jesus was an answer to Irene's childhood prayer years before when she had peered through the lattice work under the porch in Parkdale, saying, "Lord, always keep me by Your side. Always let me hear Your voice. Never let me stray away from Your will."

As autumn approached, Irene and the children continued their frequent visits to Ada in the nursing home. By now they were "regulars," stopping by to say hello to many of the other residents.

Melissa, now three years old, would climb gently into the lap of some weathered, white haired grandparent, wrap her arm around their neck and ask, in her clear child-voice, "Do you know Jesus? He's my friend, He can be your friend too. If you know Him you get to go to heaven. Isn't that neat?"

And so they ministered to the folks in the nursing home, Irene chuckling at the blessed but audacious behavior of her children.

"I wonder where they learned that?" she thought to herself.

Ada's condition began to deteriorate. She did not have Alzheimer's — but, like Irene, her thyroid production had been insufficient for many years, a condition discovered too late by medical professionals. This affected Ada's heart and contributed to a series of mini-strokes, which seriously affected her memory. She often did not know where she was, and almost never recognized Irene, thinking that Irene was her sister Delpha.

Irene knew that her time with Ada was short, but when Ada fell and broke her hip in November, she believed there would be no hope of bringing her home for Christmas. She prayed and asked the Lord for this last family time with her grandmother.

And one morning as she watched *The 700 Club* on television, Ben Kinchlow, the host at that time, stopped talking in the middle of a sentence, pointed his finger straight at the screen and said, "And a woman out there has been caring for an elderly family member and desires to take this person home for Christmas. Do so, because it will be a very memorable time, and the Lord will bless your time together."

On Christmas morning Chris drove early to Clancy Nursing Home, carried Ada from her bed and brought her home. For the first time in months she ate a normal breakfast of bacon and eggs, followed by homemade Christmas fudge. She talked to the girls. She laughed, her memory going in and out at brief intervals.

And then, for one period of time, four or five minutes long, the cloud was completely raised from her memory and she was totally coherent.

"Darlin'," she said to Irene. "Thank you for taking care of me when no one else would. I'm glad that you brought me home for Christmas. I'll never forget this."

She put her hands on Irene's face and said, "I love you, Irene. I know your mom wasn't good to you, but you've been my kid ever since you dumped out my red purse in Alaska. And there's nothing in the whole universe that will ever change that, honey."

Irene was amazed that her grandmother did not call her Delpha. She knew exactly where she was and who she was speaking to. Afterwards, she drifted back into that haze of confusion and incoherence. But those moments of clarity on the gifts that God gave Irene from her grandmother, the culmination and affirmation of affection from her childhood. This sharing from Ada's heart healed even more areas in Irene's spirit.

In the years after Chris and Irene were married, Irene and her family had kept only marginal contact. She was aware that the lives of her brothers and sisters remained strongly affected by the alcoholism and abuse in their formative years.

One by one their lives had been devastated by alcohol, drug abuse, bad marriages, and other unhappiness. Irene longed for them to know the Lord and allow His healing touch their lives. But they viewed their sister as a "holier than thou" preacher's wife, anticipating her condemnation of their lifestyles.

Irene did remain close to Laura, her second youngest sister. And when she invited family members to visit Ada in Montana, Laura came with her own daughter, Ada.

They had a wonderful visit, sister to sister, and took Grandma Ada on a picnic. They talked about some of the happy times they had as children. One morning, as they watched *The 700 Club*, a story came on about sexual abuse — the hidden, ugly secret in families.

Laura watched quietly for a while, then nonchalantly went into the bathroom. Irene waited for her, sensing that something was wrong, and when Laura came out crying, she gently broached the subject.

"Laura, I know all about it, because the same thing happened to me," Irene said.

Laura sobbed heavily and collapsed next to Irene on the couch. After 25 years, they shared with one another the horrifying abuse they had each received from their demented Grandfather Jess.

"I hope you can lay that to rest, Laura," Irene said. "Jesus has given me total peace about all this. He has healed my spirit, and

He wants to heal you too."

She gave Laura a Bible and told her how God had restored her. She told her about the visions the Lord had given her. She explained that all she had to do was just trust Him, and He would take each memory and put Himself into that memory with scriptures, just like a medicine to help the soul.

She explained how He can renew the mind by the washing of His Word, the Holy Bible, changing the nature of the bad memories — not that the memories are removed, but that the hurt is removed from the recollection. No longer do they sting and bite and tear and rip your heart out every time the incident comes to mind. The memory is never lost, because it is a part of the person. But it's a memory that's okay, because the pain is gone.

It was a unique time. Laura listened intently, but gave no obvious sign of wanting a relationship with the Lord. Irene rejoiced anyway. It was the first time she had been able to share her faith with anyone in her family. The rest had remained closed, telling Irene to shut up every time she mentioned anything about her faith in the Lord. So she had kept her faith and feelings to herself, realizing that the very light of Jesus in her heart and mind convicted them of their sin, even when she said nothing.

Irene held Laura in her prayers, and she took the matter of her sister's salvation and healing before God. He showed her that her brothers — Mike, Willy and Sam — and sisters — Shirley and Laura — had all been molested by Grandpa Jess. He opened her eyes to the clues that had been in front of her all the time. And she wept with this knowledge.

As she thought of the many powerful and horrible affects of this abuse on her family, she again fought the seed of bitterness against Jess.

Once again she thought, "It's one thing to forgive someone for hurting me, but it is another story altogether to forgive someone for hurting the ones you love."

And in this deep struggle, the Lord brought to her memory the vision of Gethsemane. Again He prayed for her, "I'll teach her to forgive." And as she gave her anger and resentment to the Lord, day by day, Jesus taught her to forgive.

Being at East Helena Foursquare Church was a unique time. God taught Chris many things about patience and abut being a pastor that doesn't make the ministry an idol in his life.

After two years of close association with the Family Life Center, Irene felt that the Lord was preparing for them to have their own congregation again. As she prayed, the Lord spoke to her once again: "I have not forgotten you. The time has not come for you to move yet. But the time is soon. I have many things to teach you, and other people, about My people and the ways I work in them. The changing of minds is not in My hands. The season is almost over. I am preparing you and Chris for a great ministry that will take great strength. I am binding you together with stronger cords, sharpening you as a man would with a stone. You are My beloved people and I have called thee forth for My purpose and that purpose will be fulfilled. Glean what you can during this time. The season is almost over. I will send you forth. You are a blessing to Me."

Soon after this prophecy, Chris and Irene received a call from Hope Chapel, a Foursquare Church in Bozeman, Montana, to fill in for the pastor while he spent a year preaching in China.

The people in East Helena Foursquare expressed their loving good-byes. In a emotional ceremony, the pastor commended them on their attitude of service. He talked about how — even when they had no place to live or food to eat — they never complained about anything. They came in the early mornings and ministered to the people despite having had no breakfast. In this attitude of love and appreciation, Chris and Irene left for Bozeman, knowing that they would always have a special place in their hearts for these loving people.

The doctor was adamant that Ada not be moved to Bozeman, and as Irene planned for people to continue to care for her grandmother, she yearned for her mother to understand her motives for bringing Ada to Montana.

On a visit to her grandmother, Irene approached one of the doctors for advice. He was already aware of some of the problems in Ada's family. She told him some of the family history and the prevalence of alcoholism and other abuse.

"Do not expect anything from your mother," he said, after some thought. "She is an alcoholic. You need to release her from the expectations you have held for her since you were a child."

Irene considered his words.

"Don't expect her to act like your mother," he continued. "Just treat her like somebody you know."

"Okay, I'll try that," she answered.

Inside Irene prayed fervently, "God please, when we go to Astoria, don't let me expect anything from my mom. Let her be free from my expectations. Show me how to treat her like anyone else I know. If that's the way our relationship has to be then that's okay with me. I let go of it all. I forgive her for every bad thing she ever did to me or my family. I hold nothing back."

Before leaving for Bozeman, the family took a brief trip to visit their families on the coast. Irene tried for several days to reach her mother, to no avail.

But one morning after praying very hard the night before, the Lord woke Irene and said clearly, "Go get your mom right away or she won't be able to spend any time with you."

"Okay, Lord," she answered.

Over the years, to their sadness, her problem with alcohol seemed to have taken complete control of her life. They rushed to pick her up, realizing that later in the day she would probably be too intoxicated to enjoy a visit.

Irene prayed over and over, "Let go of it!"

As they brought her back to the house, Evelyn's face was cheerful and happy in anticipation of a day of shopping and lunch downtown. She went upstairs with Irene, and they laughed together like teenagers, combing each other's hair and putting on makeup. Evelyn leaned over Irene in the mirror, gave her a big hug and said, "Don't we make a good pair, honey?"

Irene looked at her mother in astonishment.

"Yes, we do, Mom."

"Let's go have lunch and go shopping," Evelyn said.

Irene looked at her mother's face, considering how rarely she had seen any happiness in those eyes.

In the afternoon, laden with new shirts, shoes, and pants, gifts from Chris and Irene, they returned to the house.

"I'm in the height of my glory with all these new clothes. I can't believe this," Evelyn said, hugging Irene. "I sure love you, Irene. I'm so glad you're my daughter."

Again Irene reacted to this unexpected show of affection — the smile and the approval lighting up her mother's face.

At lunch, Evelyn turned to Irene and said, "You know, I've been awful hard on you about trying to help Grandma."

"I know, Mom."

"How is she?"

"She's okay. When we went to visit her, she didn't know who we were, but I have somebody take care of her a few times a week. They let us know how she's doing."

"I'm really glad that you helped Grandma like you did. I knew I couldn't do it."

By now it was time to go back.

"I want to fix a good dinner for you and Chris and the kids. Drop me off at Laura's house. You guys come back in an hour and we'll all have dinner together."

An hour later, Chris, Irene, the children, Mike, Laura, Ruth, Willy, and Evelyn sat down together for the first time in more than 15 years. The table was loaded with food — turkey and dressing that Laura had started preparing earlier, combined with Evelyn's salads and other goodies. They ate and laughed and joked together. It was a wonderful time.

When the evening was over, Chris and Irene took Evelyn back to her apartment. She hugged each of the girls and kissed them. Then she turned to Irene.

"I love you, Reenie. You're such a good mom. I'm so proud of you." She hugged Irene and continued, "You're such a blessing to me, my shining star. Never forget that."

And then they left.

It had been a day of firsts. She could not remember ever shopping with her mother, or sitting down to a peaceful meal without the angry influence of alcohol bringing on a fight with someone.

She searched her mind to remember if her mother had ever before told her that she loved or even liked her. In all the years she could remember only a couple of times. Never had Evelyn said that she approved of Irene or that she had turned out to be a good mother.

In that one day, God gave her the immeasurable blessing of hearing all the positive things she needed to hear from her mother. As she let go of her expectations, it was as though her judgments had melted away. And as her mother sensed that Irene no longer held disapproval for her, she was free to love her daughter without reservation. As Irene released that control, she finally learned how to forgive, deep inside, and let go of all those past hurts — to realize that her mother was an alcoholic and that no one but Jesus could do anything to change her. In His eyes, all sins are equal. Only human pride allows one sinner to feel superior, wrongly comparing the "quality" of their sins.

Now she could also see the paralyzing power of fear in Evelyn's life, her not knowing how to give love and then not loving because she didn't want to get it wrong. Instead of taking the risk, her mother held back from both giving and receiving affection, keeping her pride intact in that lonely, protected place.

"Thank you, Lord Jesus, for showing me once again the power of forgiveness," Irene prayed. "Set the captives free, Lord. Save my family, every one of them. And repair the damage from our past — all of us."

BOZEMAN

No man shall be able to stand before you all the days of your life. As I was with Moses, so I will be with you; I will not fail you or forsake you. Be strong [confident], and of good courage, for you shall cause this people to inherit the land, which I swore to their fathers to give them.

Joshua 1:5,6 AMP

Blessed — happy, fortunate, prosperous and enviable — is the man who walks and lives not in the counsel of the ungodly [following their advice, their plans and purposes], nor stands [submissive and inactive] in the path where sinners walk, nor sits down [to relax and rest] where the scornful [and the mockers] gather. But his delight and desire are in the law of the Lord, and on His law — the precepts, the instructions, the teachings of God — he habitually meditates (ponders and studies) by day and by night.

Psalm 1:1,2 AMP

From the time of their marriage in Astoria until the move to Bozeman in 1986, Chris, Irene, and the children had moved 14 times. And so once again, they re-established themselves into a borrowed house, placing all their belongings in storage.

Irene wondered again why God continued to deny her deep

desire to have her own home. And as she prayed, He showed her that His purpose stemmed from His desire to heal her from the affects of her dysfunctional background. At this point, it was still too easy for her to fall into the trap of placing her trust in material possessions. And as she trusted the Lord more and more, He matured her faith.

> *I will instruct thee and teach thee in the way which thou shalt go. And I will guide thee with mine eye. Be not like as a horse or a mule which have no understanding, whose mouth must be held in a bit and a bridle, lest they come near unto thee. Many sorrows shall be to the wicked; but he that trusteth in the Lord, mercy shall compass him about. Be glad in the Lord, and rejoice, ye righteous; and shout for joy, all ye that are upright in heart.*
>
> Psalms 32:8-11 KJV

In the next year the Lord continued to teach Chris and Irene about being pastors. Chris became more adept at delegating work, learning not to bear the entire burden of church "business" on his own shoulders.

The Lord began to show Irene that many of the "rules" set down in the etiquette class at Bible school were not His rules. There was no set pattern of behavior for a pastor's wife when she is submitted to her husband and to the Lordship of Jesus.

The Lord showed them that everything they received from Him as a word of knowledge — things that He spoke to their hearts — should be tested against the Bible. In the Lord, there would be no contradiction of His direction. Together she and Chris learned new freedom in their faith.

As Irene struggled to understand what was expected of her as a pastor's wife, the Lord gave her a dream that took her back to her childhood. Once again she sat in the tiny rocking chair in Grandpa Ernie's house, tying the laces on her new red and white patent leather shoes. She remembered the stabbing pain of his rejection as he saw that the shoes were on the wrong feet.

"Can't you get anything right, Irene?"

She remembered the rejection of his displeasure, the feeling that she would do absolutely anything to earn his approval.

And as the dream memory faded, the Lord spoke to her: "That is the mentality that you have when anybody in authority is around you. Always wanting to please people. Irene, I want to use you, even if you do not know your left from your right, even if you make mistakes. My love for you is not dependent on your behavior."

> *But now in Christ Jesus ye who sometimes were far off are made nigh by the blood of Christ. For He is our peace, who hath made both one and hath broken down the middle wall of partition between us; . . . And that he might reconcile both unto God in one body by the cross, having slain the enmity thereby . . . Now therefore ye are no more strangers and foreigners, but fellow citizens with the saints, and of the household of God.*
>
> Ephesians 2:13,14,19 KJV

He reminded her once again of the picture He had given her of the dresser.

"I will complete this work that I have begun in you. I will continue to clean out those drawers and repair the brokenness in your life. But I will decide when to deal with these things.

"I want to get to the root of the problems, the unseen motives. I want to get rid of the grudges you have held for the things done to people you love. I want you to examine your motives in holding those grudges and to help you let go of all those things.

"I do not ask you to trust those people, just to forgive them.

"As I bring these things to your mind, Irene, I will ask if you are ready to deal with that memory. It is up to you. But remember that when you hold on to things that I am ready to heal, it only prolongs the pain for you and delays the healing."

Looking back, Irene could see the hand of God carefully mending the memories of her past and removing the pain. Each morning as she rose to dress and took her clothing out of the dresser she remembered this picture God had given her. Piece by piece He was healing her.

It had been a wonderful year for the family. They rode bicycles and ran, enjoying the fresh air and exercise. Together they fished, swam and climbed the steep mountains that surrounded the lovely city of Bozeman. The church prospered and their lives seemed blessed beyond compare.

At the end of the year the regular pastor returned from China. When Chris and Irene turned to the Lord about their future, two prophesies were given.

During a communion service at the church the Lord said, "I have a home for you. It is not the first place that you will go. The first place will be very hard, but you will only stay for a short time. The second place that I will send you, you will see the fruit of your ministry. And you will have a home. It will be hard at first, and it will take a long time to see the fruit, but it will come. Do not give up on the promise that I have given you."

In a second prophecy, the Lord reiterated His promise, "Remember that I can make flowers bloom in the desert."

Never had the concept of spiritual warfare seemed so real. It was obvious that the difficult training ground in Helena had been to prepare them to handle an even more strenuous position. A few weeks later, they received the call to Weiser, Idaho.

Just before moving, they went to collect their belongings from the garage in Helena, only to find that water had soaked through a hole in the roof and destroyed nearly all of their possessions. As Chris and Irene surveyed the soggy pile, they noticed a piece of plastic covering a box of keepsake pictures of their children.

Irene was deeply distressed. Painful childhood memories haunted her, and she ask the Lord to supply the necessary furnishings for her home.

As she took these hurts to the Lord, He gently quieted her spirit and reminded her, "Even if you do not have a chair to sit on, you always have a place to sit with Me that will last for eternity. Chairs will fade and grow old, and you will have to throw them away, but the chair I have for you will last for eternity."

Peace poured over her spirit like warm honey, soothing her troubled soul. As she relinquished the fear to her Lord, her heart regained the joy that He promised.

Later that month their house in Astoria sold after being on the market for two years. Now they had money to buy beds for the children and some modest furniture for their home in Weiser.

WEISER

I have told you these things so that in Me you may have perfect peace and confidence. In the world you have tribulation and trials and distress and frustration; but be of good cheer — take courage, be confident, certain undaunted — for I have overcome the world. — I have deprived it of power to harm, have conquered it [for you].

John 16:33 AMP

I was living at ease, but [Satan] crushed me and broke me apart; yes, he seized me by the neck and dashed me in pieces, then set me up for his target. [Satan's] arrows whiz around me; he slashes open my vitals, and does not spare; he pours out my gall on the ground. [Satan] stabs me, making breach after breach and attacking again and again; he runs at me like a giant and irresistible warrior. I have sewed sackcloth over my skin [as a sign of mourning], and have defiled my horn — my [insignia of] strength — in the dust. My face is red and swollen with weeping, and on my eyelids is the shadow of death — my eyes are dimmed; Although there is no guilt or violence in my hands, and my prayer is pure. O earth, cover not my blood, and let my cry have no resting place where it will cease being heard[. Even now, behold my Witness is in Heaven, and He who vouches for me is on high. My friends scorn me, but my eye pours out tears to God. O that there were one who might plead for a man with God and that he would maintain his right with Him, as a son of man pleads with or for his neighbor!

Job 16:12-21 AMP

Candle in the Wind

I'm just a candle
A candle in the wind
I'm just a candle
A candle in the wind
Just a flicker of light
In this world of night
Can my life make a difference for Him.

So many times I want to run and hide
And say Lord, not me, O Lord
It's dark, it's dark outside
If I stand real still
No one knows I'm real
It hurts to be your candle in the wind.

I'll be your candle
Your candle in the wind
I'll be your candle
Your candle in the wind
Just a flicker of light
In this world of night
Can my life make a difference for Him.

The world would say
Turn out your light
You're burning much too bright
So I just turn and go
But Jesus said to me
I have set you free
I've bought you with a price.

I'll be your lampstand
Your lampstand.
I'll hold you through the night

I'll be your lampstand
Your lampstand.
I'll keep you burning bright
Just a flicker of light
In this world of night.
Yes your life makes a difference to me.
Yes your life makes a difference to me.

Irene Taylor

Opening the door to their new home, their eyes lit upon a table covered with flowers and finger foods. A huge card signed with more than 60 names delivered a hearty welcome to the family. It was a joyful homecoming and it seemed their new life in Weiser was off to a good start.

Weiser, a small farming town near the border of Idaho and Oregon, sits in a valley surrounded by acres of onion and beet fields. The congregation was small and the church could afford only a moderate income for their pastor. For entertainment the local people went to the grocery store and sat on benches, watching people walk by.

With all the children but Melissa in school, Irene decided to find some work to supplement the family income. Leaving Melissa with Chris, she got a job three days a week packing the weeds used in dried flower arrangements. She worked on a large farm just outside of town. She loved being in the sun and fresh air.

Irene got into their old blue car about 5:30 a.m. and picked weeds until 2:30 p.m. She was young, healthy and fast, able to cut about 40 bundles a day. And at a dollar per bundle, it seemed a fairly easy way to make money.

For several weeks that summer, the prophecy, "The first place will be a short period of time, a very hard place," did not seem to ring true. The church prospered and the children thrived in the new environment.

As summer wore on, the crews completed harvesting the weed crop and many of the workers moved on to garner onions. Irene's job was to stand at the head of the conveyor belt and begin the sorting process, separating the pungent vegetables by size, color, and quality. This work was different in nature. No longer was she out in the fresh breezy air. Her eyes and nostrils burned with the caustic odor of onion. Instead of walking through the fields, she now stood still on legs that ached hour after hour. Many of the other women spoke Spanish, and she felt left out of their friendly conversation.

As the harvest ended, Irene felt very ill. She had a rash on the back of her right leg which was swollen and almost as painful as her enlarged hands. At times she could barely move her fingers and hard bumps formed around the joints. She also felt nauseous.

In October the doctor told her that she probably had rheumatoid arthritis, continuing from the juvenile arthritis she had as a child. The arthritis in her leg, probably inflamed by an allergy to the onions, was making her body swell. He recommended knee surgery to repair some damaged cartilage and to reduce the arthritis, but had no solution for her other problems. Irene told him that they had no insurance, and asked to delay surgery. He put her on anti-inflammatory medication and gave her a leg brace.

For the next few months, she wore the ankle to hip steel brace, walking straight legged up and down stairs. Her leg throbbed. It seemed worse with the brace.

In November, Irene had a ruptured ovarian cyst. On examination this doctor became convinced that she had cervical cancer and needed a hysterectomy immediately. Irene gritted her teeth, prayed harder, and entered the hospital in January to have both the knee surgery and a partial hysterectomy at the same time. Post surgical tests revealed a pre-cancerous condition, but the problem seemed to have been resolved by the surgery.

But Irene's health did not improve after the operations. Ten days after leaving the hospital, while Chris had gone to work and Emily, Amanda, and Christy trudged off to school, Irene and Melissa sat quietly coloring. Suddenly Irene was overwhelmed with a sudden blinding headache. The pain doubled her over, and she closed her eyes against the light. In a few moments she opened them again and the sight above mid-level in her left eye had faded to black. She carefully controlled her reaction to the pain and blindness, trying not to frighten Melissa. Any movement of her head produced sharp, shooting pains through her eyes, and down into her arms and legs. She felt an increasing heaviness and spasms of pain in her chest. Her rib cage felt like it was being crushed. Her left arm felt strange and she was unable to move it above her head.

"Melissa, get the telephone book for Mommy," she said, carefully controlling her voice. But she could not see to read the numbers. Carefully and slowly she directed Melissa to find the number for her surgeon.

At first, her doctor sounded unconcerned.

"You just had surgery. You have probably gotten a touch of the flu, there is nothing wrong with you. If you are still feeling like this later on in the afternoon, come in to the office."

By 4 p.m. the chest pains had increased in severity, and Irene was sure she was having a heart attack. Unable to reach Chris, she called a neighbor to take her to the doctor.

As he began his preliminary examination, he became very serious. "You don't feel good, do you?"

"No, that's what I said earlier today."

He gave her a balance test, finding that she could barely stand without holding on to something, and she could not walk a straight line. And after completing a test of her peripheral vision, and counting a heartbeat of around 45, he dialed 911 from his office.

"Your lungs are full; it could be pneumonia," he said into her fear filled face. "You need to go to the hospital right away. You either have a blood clot in your lungs or one in your brain. Or you may have MS, multiple sclerosis. Do you want the helicopter "Life Flight" or do you think you can stand the ambulance ride into Boise?"

As he gave instructions to the emergency personnel over the telephone, Irene's mind raced. As he hung up, she hit him with a flurry of questions.

"MS? How could I have MS? I just had surgery. I never had it before." She was breathless with anxiety.

"Sometimes major illness or sickness can bring on attack of MS or an underlying disease that you have had for a long time. Your body cannot fight off that and simultaneously heal itself after surgery. But if that is what it is, we'll deal with it when we have to."

So Irene left the doctor's office in an ambulance, praying all the way to Boise.

At school, the principal told Christy that her mom had been

taken away in an ambulance. She sat down on the floor and cried, sure that her mother was going to die. Irene also thought she was dying.

The numerous tests at St. Alphonsus Hospital were inconclusive. She was examined by a neurologist who confirmed her symptoms, but could find no decisive reason for her blindness, pain, and muscle failure. Her MRI scan was inconclusive and the neurologist told her that she could be suffering from stress or multiple sclerosis. And after several days, the doctors gave Irene nitroglycerin for her continuing heart pain and sent her home, still suffering from the pounding headaches, failing eyesight, and difficulty breathing.

Chris and Irene were at a loss. Of all the spiritual difficulties they had imagined after the prophecy, the loss of Irene's health had not been expected. They poured over scripture, prayed without ceasing, pleading for a cure as the hospital bills accumulated. The tests did not confirm a diagnosis of multiple sclerosis.

During the next months, Irene lost vision in her other eye, had a constant sore throat, painful diarrhea, vomiting, joint pain in her shoulders, neck, and jaw, dizziness, extreme fatigue, and weight gain. Many days she could barely get out of bed.

Church members rallied around the family, providing support and help of different kinds as days turned into weeks and Irene showed no improvement.

At first, Chris was understanding and patient, as any loving husband would be. But as the pressures mounted he felt an increasing sense of rage, at the situation, at Irene, at the disease, at God. Now his daily schedule included all Irene's chores, plus his pastoral duties. He rose early to prepare breakfast for the children. He did the laundry, ironed his shirts, cleaned the house, fed all the pets, and tried to provide support for his afflicted wife.

But more than all else, he missed her running with him up the hillsides, gathering wildflowers for an impromptu bouquet, listening to his rambling stories about his day. In her pain it seemed that these intimacies were beyond their reach.

The children tried to bear parts of the burden. Irene directed them in brushing one another's hair and buttoning difficult clothing. Her heart ached as they strained to complete a task that would have been nothing to her before her illness.

As Chris watched her frustration, the Lord showed him the powerful influence of chronic illness on a family. Now he saw Irene's illness almost as a demon striving for control over their family. And as he prayed, the Lord showed him the importance of not allowing the illness to dominate their lives.

"Take charge over this illness. Do not let it take charge over you," the Lord told him.

And so he strived to maintain a normal life in the midst of his wife's increasing loss of function.

By March, Irene could walk, supported by a wall, but the pain was excruciating. Every joint in her body screamed against the effort. She grew increasingly angry at God: "God, you heal other people. Why don't you heal me? I have prayed for people with MS, and You totally healed them. And I don't understand why. If I'm supposed to be Your servant and I'm supposed to be Your child, why am I left to have MS the rest of my life — never being normal, or able to sweep my floor or brush my hair? I just don't like this God. It's just not right."

As she struggled with the spiritual side of her illness, well-meaning people from church told her that she simply did not have enough faith to get well.

"If you trusted God enough, He would heal you this very minute. It is your lack of faith that keeps you sick."

"Where on earth did you get that idea?" Irene asked.

"Well, the Bible says if you have the faith as a grain of mustard seed you could move a mountain. Or you must have some hidden sin in your life. Or else you are harboring unforgiveness toward someone."

Irene looked at them, trying to control her anger.

"The Bible also recognizes the supreme sovereignty of Almighty God. Isaiah 45:6-7 says, "I am the Lord, and there is no other. I form the light and create darkness, I bring prosperity and create disaster; I, the Lord, do all these things."

She pointed out time after time in the New Testament when Jesus healed people who did not even know Him.

"I have no lack of faith," she said. "God could heal me and every person on this earth this very minute if He wanted to. I don't have a doubt of that in my mind. How dare you suggest that healing is in my hands. Do you think God is a respecter of persons?

Do you think He heals one of His children and not the other because of what they do or say? That is ridiculous! God is not a vending machine that you put a quarter in and get the candy bar. He is my Father. He loves me, and He will heal me in His time and for His purpose."

After they left, she turned to the Lord, and He confirmed what she had told them.

"Some people make a god of faith," He said. "They worship the idea of faith. I have said, 'Thou shalt have no other gods before me.' And I will not have them making a god of faith. I am Almighty God. Do not substitute *anything* else for Me."

"I understand, Lord. But please tell me, God, how am I going to deal with all this pain all the time? I can't live on pain pills the rest of my life."

And once again the Lord gave her a prescription: "In springtime you're going to be a lot better, Irene."

And as she listened and waited on the Lord, He began to sing to her:

> *My beloved's face is precious to me.*
> *Rise up my love, my fair one and come away.*
> *For lo the winter is over and gone.*
> *Flowers appear on the earth.*
> *The time of the singing of birds has come*
> *And the turtle dove is heard in our land.*

The lovely chorus stayed in her heart and mind for days, bringing her a renewed sense of peace and soothing her pain. But when she told Chris about the Lord's promise, his first thought was: "Which spring, Lord?"

Even in her sickness she still felt an obsession to perform her duties in the ministries. With her head splitting, she forced herself to sing on Sunday mornings. She tried with all her might to block the pain by saying, "Okay God, remember when I told you that I thought I was going to die, You gave me the scripture:

> *The captive exile and he who is bent down by chains*
> *shall speedily be released, and he **shall not die** and*
> *go down to the pit of destruction, nor shall his food*
> *fail. For I am the Lord your God, Who stirs up the*

sea so that its waves roar, and by rebuke restrains it.
*The Lord of hosts is His name. And **I have put My***
words in your mouth and have covered you in the
***shadow of My hand**, that I may fix the new heavens*
as a tabernacle, and lay the foundations of a new
earth, and say to Zion, You are My people.

Isaiah 51:14-16 AMP

"You promised that I was not going to die."

As these days of pain blended into one lengthening agony, she retained fragments of memories: Chris putting on her makeup, brushing her hair, helping with her shoes. Eventually she could no longer stand at the kitchen sink to wash dishes or sweep with a broom. The pain in her joints worsened — until all she could do was sit on the couch or stay in bed.

She missed her grandmother terribly, feeling as though they had abandoned her, moving first to Bozeman, and now to Weiser. But Ada no longer recognized the family, and the doctor told Irene that the move would kill her. So she checked on her weekly by phone, wishing she felt well enough to drive to Helena.

Relations remained strained between Irene and her family, and the eventual death of Ada did nothing to alleviate tensions. As Irene's illness progressed, she and Chris were confused as to what they should tell her family. There was still no diagnosis, only the continuing devastating symptoms.

But the hand of God moves in mysterious ways.

As Irene's illness was brought before their congregation in Weiser, individuals took her need for prayer with them to other churches. Word spread from believer to believer, covering her illness with prayer and intercession to Almighty God.

As the word spread, a couple from Astoria who had been on vacation in Idaho returned to their home church and requested prayer for this ailing pastor's wife in Weiser, Idaho. Little did they know that Irene's younger sister Laura sat in stunned silence in the congregation. She was totally ignorant of her sister's life and death struggle.

In this way God informed her family of her illness.

They began to call her, at first hesitantly, then regularly, as they realized how truly ill she was. Irene's heart was so warmed by the increasing affection, she could hardly believe what was happening. First her sisters and brothers, and then even her mother began to call to ask how she was, to care for her.

Within a few months, the family moved from their small dwelling into a nicer house with bedrooms for each of the children. It was a pleasant little place, next to a green pasture with horses and sheep.

Chris continued with his determination that the family would not be ruled by Irene's unnamed disease. They got a little dog to keep her company while the family went on with normal life. Irene joined in the activities whenever she felt well enough.

The dog, Tilly, was a little, perfectly behaved terrier with sweet, laughing eyes. And Irene loved to sit and talk to her, charmed by her lady-like manners and personality. Now, when Chris and the girls went fishing, or on some other outing inevitably leaving Irene to patiently wait for their return, she would hold in her tears until they left and talk out the pain to the loving little dog. She staunchly defended her family's need to remain as normal as possible, but as they left her alone to run off to school functions or on outings in the summer weather, her heart would break to be so left out. Tilly would lay in her arms and reach up to lick wet tears off her face.

One afternoon she hung onto the side of the house and tottered along to the back fence. There, as she propped herself against the wooden slats and looked up into the sky, the Lord said, "In Isaiah I said, 'They that wait upon the Lord shall renew their strength. They shall mount up with wings like eagles. They shall run and not be weary. They shall walk and not faint.'"

And she answered, "Please teach me, Lord, to wait on You."

As she listened once again, the Lord sang to her:

> Though weeping lasts for a night,
> Joy comes in the morning.
> Hold on my child, joy comes in the morning.
> The darkest hour means dawn is just in sight.
> To give the things you cannot keep,
> For what you cannot lose.
> Is the way to find the joy
> God has for you.

And she asked, "I just wish there was an end. God, if you're not going to take me home, please heal me."

But He continued singing the song to her as she wept and wept. It was not the crying of sadness, but it was a wail from the depths of a broken heart. She wanted so much for God to change her circumstances. She felt like her life was fading to nothing, like smoke dissipating into thin air — the foreboding of impending death.

Each day seemed to take one more part of life away from her. She watched Chris push the girls on their bicycles as they learned how to ride. She was a bystander, a non-participant in the lives of her own children.

Melissa prepared to start kindergarten, and Irene wanted to walk the six blocks to take her down to school. But the effort and pain were too much for her.

As she watched her youngest daughter get ready for her first day of school, Melissa turned to catch her mother observing her with intense sadness.

"Mommy, if you need for me to stay home with you another year, I will."

"No, that's okay, honey."

Then Melissa brought Mr. Puffalump, her favorite stuffed animal to her mother and tucked him carefully into her arms.

"You can have him to hug until I get back. Okay, Mommy?"

Irene thought her heart would break.

She identified strongly with Joni Earickson-Tada, with the endless pain and isolation she endured after the accident that left her paralyzed. She listened over and over to a tape from Joni about dealing with depression and physical problems. For months, Joni lay in bed while nurses rotated her body to avoid bed sores. She told about being so mad at God because He wouldn't heal her. But Joni, too, had been given an experience similar to Irene's when she danced with the Lord. It was a secret place that the Lord made for her. A personal retreat for the times that the pain was too much to bear.

In times like these, the Lord would remind Irene, "Go back to that place where you danced in heaven with Me. Take the little things, whatever you *can* do today, and use that to sustain you."

Little Things

Little things mean so much
Smiles from people you don't know
Rainbows from God in the morning

Baby's laugh, cat's meow, and rain on your face—
A flower just ready to bloom
Kind words from a friend
A phone call from your sister

A clay pot a little girl made just for you
Songs about Jesus
A kiss of Son light
On a cloudy day
Oh, thank you, God, for the little things
You let me see.

Irene Taylor

Later that summer Chris and Irene prepared to celebrate their fifteenth wedding anniversary. They left the girls at Chris' parents' house in Bellingham, Washington, and drove down the coast to Astoria. They had a marvelous time, bittersweet with undercurrents that it might be Irene's last trip. It was the first time in years they had spent without the children or the every day pressures of running a church.

Between long walks on the beach and romantic dinners, they visited Irene's stepfather William at home with his wife, Ramona. It was a joyful reunion, and they spent several hours catching up on one another's lives. Many good things had happened to William through the intervening years, but there were also many painful memories.

As they sat talking in his living room, William told them about his brother Lyle. Irene remembered the magical times she had spent on Lyle's ranch, the wonderful food, clean clothing and horseback riding. In his home she had reveled in clean sheets, and the peaceful sober conversations at meal times. She remembered her uncle going out of his way to get the children to their own church each Sunday. He was a wonderful man of God.

Lyle had been called to the mission field in Kenya and served for a year working in the fields of the Lord. William remembered how happy his brother had been, knowing that his life had meaning and purpose.

But as the politicos of Kenya had increased in power and hatred of foreign influence in their country, Lyle's ministry and his life were threatened. In the end, Lyle was imprisoned for a period and then released. As he waited one afternoon for permission to build wells for fresh water, he received notification that he would be returned to prison for "supposedly" supplying munitions to rebel forces. The shock was too much, and he had slumped over, dying immediately of a heart attack. It was a numbing blow to William.

Grandpa Jess had also passed away. Irene told William that during one of their summer visits to the coast she had been able to talk to Jess about Jesus, that she hoped that he had been saved. But she did not tell her step-father about the years of abuse at the hands of his own father. There was no point in hurting him further in the face of the loss of these two men he loved.

And as they shared in his grief, William began to cry, his attention wandering over other painful memories in his life.

"I wish that I could have been the kind of dad I was supposed to be. There are so many things I could have fixed," he said.

"Honey, I'm sorry about the fire," he continued. "I wish I could change the way I handled that situation. I've always known the fire wasn't your fault. I hope you can forgive me."

"Daddy, I forgive you."

Then he hugged her and kissed her cheek saying, "I'm so sorry that you're so sick."

"It's okay, Dad. Jesus is with me, and He makes the pain bearable. Maybe He will heal me — or at least let the doctors find out what's wrong and start treatment. God promised me it would be okay."

"I just don't understand life sometimes, why such a good man as my brother Lyle, who loved God, and feared God, could die on the mission field. I don't understand things about God. And I don't understand why you have to be sick. Why is that?"

"Daddy, you know, we probably wouldn't be having this conversation if I weren't sick, would we?"

"No."

"God's ways are not our ways," she said, looking into his tired, sad face, "but if I had to get sick to have this talk that I'm having with you today, it is all worth it. It's all worth it! Have you ever accepted Jesus, Dad?"

"Yes, I have."

"Do you know for a fact that you have Jesus in your heart? Because I know that Uncle Lyle, with his dying breath wanted more than anything for you to know Jesus."

"I know, Irene."

"Well, do you, Dad?"

"Jesus has never been a problem with me. It's religion. People are always putting this religious stuff on me. You have to wear a certain kind of clothes, talk a certain way, go to church every Sunday, and all those kinds of things."

"I don't like religion much either, Dad. It's kept too many people away from God. All you have to do is have Jesus in your heart and accept what He did on the cross, and you're saved. It's a relationship between Jesus and you, as your friend. Know without a doubt that He died on the cross for you. It doesn't matter if you ever step into a church, as long as you know that."

He put his arm around her and laid his head on her shoulder.

"Honey, I do know that."

She smiled and held him tight, feeling at last the release from worrying about William. Joy welled up in her heart.

"I love your laugh, Dad. I love the way you told us stories when we were kids, and I love the way that you tried to take care of us. Thank you."

And with these parting words, Chris and Irene left. It was the best conversation she had had with her father in her entire life.

During the long drive home, Irene sat in silence, pondering the incredible healing in her relationship with her step-father. She reflected on the hard times God had brought her through, and how he had used almost every negative event to bridge a gap with someone, to help them know Him better.

None of those troubling incidents was forgotten by God. In her mind she could imagine that He had each detail carefully written down waiting for an occasion to use it. Not that he hadn't designed her hardships for later use, but that he refused to waste any raw material.

All things work together for good, to them who love
God and are called according to His purpose.

Romans 8:28 NIV

The enemy had chosen to sift her life like wheat. But the Lord took every bad grain and made it into life, like a human compost heap invested with garbage, but harvesting brilliant roses. He took things that, if left alone, were based on death and devastation and turned them into life, Irene's life.

Days turned into weeks, then months, as Chris watched over Irene, tormented by the thought of her pain. Irene learned to live in smaller segments of time, getting through moment by moment. Many doctors were consulted, but all seemed to agree that either the illness was all in Irene's head, or she had some kind of muscular sclerosis. None of the tests verified a diagnosis. At times Irene wondered if they were right — had she lost her mind in some nightmare of pain?

Shortly after school started she was encouraged to start the powerful medication normally given for multiple sclerosis. But as she prayed, she felt the Lord did not want her to take the pills. She struggled, not knowing whether to follow the advice of her physician or trust the voice that she hoped and prayed was the Lord's. At times, she doubted whether she heard Him at all. But she did not take the medication.

In November, 11 months into her illness, the Lord quickened her spirit one evening as she watched television. It was as though He tapped her on the shoulder as *20/20*, the news magazine, came on, saying "Pay attention, Irene!"

One of the stories was about Lyme disease. As the article progressed, she listened with full attention as the reporter described each symptom of her affliction: severe fatigue, fever, headache, swollen lymph glands, blindness, inflamed joints with excruciating pain, especially in the knee, elbow and shoulder, dizziness, double vision, aversion to light, impaired concentration, faulty memory, nerve damage, carpal tunnel syndrome, vertigo, electrical blockage in the heart leading to slow pulse and irregular heartbeat. The list went on and on, but she had most of the symptoms.

It was quite common, the story continued, for Lyme disease to be misdiagnosed as Parkinson's or multiple sclerosis. The sickness, commonly contracted from the bite of a tick, could usually be treated if caught in the early stages, but a delay in therapy could result in irreversible damage to a variety of body systems.

The bite of a tick. Irene searched her memory trying to recall if she had received such a bite. And as the report continued it told of the characteristic rash appearing around the area of the bite. The rash is often confused with an insect bite or poison ivy.

She remembered the rash on her right leg, which had itched and swelled, adding to the pain in her aching limbs as she worked in the onion fields.

"That's it!" she cried. "That's what's wrong with me! Thank you, Lord Jesus, for showing me the truth."

Chris took her to the library and they gathered further research, praying that God would give additional confirmation of the diagnosis He had showed her.

Each additional piece of information they found only confirmed her suspicions. But now she faced the delicate problem of broaching the subject with her physician. She was more than aware that doctors resent patients who delve into self diagnosis. But she was positive that the Lord had led her to watch the television show and see the truth.

"Lord, how can I find a doctor who will get to the bottom of my disease? My doctor thinks the pain is either in my head or MS, and he can't do anything. Show me where to go. Guide me to someone who will help me get well. Please, Jesus."

As her eyesight continued to fail, Irene asked Chris if she could go to an ophthalmologist. New glasses might also help with her blinding headaches. Chris agreed. The eye doctor was quite concerned with the condition of her sight, and sent her to another specialist, where she again related the story of her assorted health problems that had appeared following her double surgery.

"Well, I know it's not all in my head," she said, daring the doctor to disagree.

The doctor looked at her incredulously, "You can't cause nerve damage like you have on the side of your face and in your eye with your head. Nerve damage is a physical phenomenon. Who told you any of this was in your head?"

As she told him about the problems she had in finding a doctor who would pursue a diagnosis of her illness, he just shook his head. He gave her the names of two other doctors.

By now Irene was burnt out on doctors. The bills continued to pour in and no one had made any progress toward a diagnosis or treatment.

She prayed, "God, if I go to another doctor who won't help me, I don't know what I'm going to do."

And the Lord said, "Ask your friend Robin about her doctor." Her doctor was one of the two suggested by the eye specialist. With this confirmation, she made the call.

Irene prayed hourly until the appointment, begging the Lord to intervene and lead the doctor to an appropriate diagnosis. At the appointment, she once again related her numerous symptoms, but carefully avoided any mention of the story on *20/20* or her knowledge of Lyme disease. In her frustration, she began to weep. Between the pain and disappointment about the lack of a diagnosis, her tears would not stop.

"He is really going to think I'm an emotional basket case," she thought, discouragement beginning before she could even complete her history. But to her astonishment, the doctor came over and put his hand on her shoulder.

"Irene, I think you have Lyme disease, not MS." As he spoke, a glimmer of hope lit in her heart. "I just have a feeling about this. The wife of one of my colleagues suffers from Lyme. It is a terrible disease. He is a neurologist, and I want you to see him immediately."

"The tests for Lyme are not readily available," he continued, "so it may take a month or two to get on top of things. I believe you're going to make it, Irene. It's going to be all right."

Irene could scarcely believe her ears. All the way home she repeated his words of hope over in her head. At last the months of waiting would come to an end. He had known about Lyme disease without her even mentioning it. He did not think her symptoms were in her head. He gave her medications for her painful symptoms — and although she had received no promise of a cure or even treatment, she was ecstatic!

Two months later the doctor called and verified the diagnosis of Lyme disease. And on March 20, the second spring after the disease took root, she began treatment.

A three-inch Heparin lock was inserted into her arm to ease

the administration of powerful intravenous antibiotics. Every day for two weeks she went to the emergency room to receive the medication. But on the third day of treatment her condition was dramatically worse. She could not walk at all, was almost totally blind, and experienced violent nausea.

"This is the reaction I've been waiting for," the doctor said. "The tests for Lyme are not totally conclusive. But a patient with true Lyme disease will always have a violent reaction to the medication as it attacks the infection."

He continued, "We will continue the treatments unless your condition becomes life threatening. Without the treatments there is a good chance you're going to die. These antibiotics will save your life."

And so she hung on knowing that, as God had promised, everything was going to be all right.

Three weeks after the treatment, her vision partially returned and her swollen joints began to normalize. She got up, washed the dishes, combed her own hair, and helped the children prepare for school. Then she walked with Melissa six blocks to kindergarten.

And she could read the Bible again. As an awareness of the extent of her returning health overwhelmed her one morning, she knelt. From the depths of her heart she thanked God for giving her life back again.

"Just antibiotics, Lord," she prayed. "What a wonderful medicine you gave us in antibiotics."

Irene's family continued to call. In the late weeks of spring, Irene began to pray for a complete reconciliation with her mother, realizing that her illness had made an opening in the rift between them. She prayed with all her heart that the Lord would heal the broken relationships in her family and bring every one of them into a relationship with Him.

She remembered the vision she had seen of Jesus in the Garden of Gethsemane.

"I'll teach her to forgive, Father," He had said.

In her heart she believed that she had forgiven her mother for the abuse and neglect she had experienced as a child. And yet, as she thought of the painful realities of their childhood, she still experienced anger, not always for herself, but for her siblings.

"How do I let go of it, Lord? She allowed horrible things to happen to us. And yet my heart cries out to know and love her, to have a real mother like other people around me. Lord, do you rewrite history? Make it like it never happened? How does forgiveness really work?"

Irene's health steadily improved during the spring. By now it had been almost two years since she had driven a car or gone anywhere unescorted, for fear that she would fall. Each day brought new freedom from pain and increased energy. She dared to hope that the suffering was over.

In May, Evelyn called and for the first time since Chris and Irene had left Oregon, and asked to visit the family. Chris carefully considered the potential effect of her visit on his young children and set down two stipulations: that she would be allowed only one six-pack of beer during her entire visit and that she would not to smoke inside the house. If she were willing to abide by those rules, she was more than welcome to come. She accepted the conditions and boarded a bus for the 12-hour ride to Weiser.

The changes in Evelyn's behavior were extraordinary. She was kind and loving to the children, giving them praise and hugging them. She offered them advice on their studies and talked to Chris for hours about his faith. Irene watched with growing fascination at the changes God was bringing into her mother's life.

For the first few days, they spent time getting to know one another again and playing with the children. They cooked meals together, went shopping, sang songs, and enjoyed each other's company. Evelyn sewed new clothes for the girls. And the whole family went fishing.

It was the longest time Irene had ever spent with her mother without her being drunk. She was overjoyed.

On the third morning, when the girls left for school, Irene walked Melissa to her first grade classroom. When she returned, Evelyn was standing in the kitchen in her nightgown pouring a cup of coffee.

"Come on Reenie, let's go out on the back porch and have a good visit."

"Okay, Momma. Do you want anything for breakfast now?"

"No, I'll just have my cup of coffee," Evelyn said, "and we can talk about things."

"Okay, Mom." Irene fought down the nervousness in her heart. "Please Lord, let us have a good visit."

As Irene settled into a comfortable chair, her mother began to sing one of the old songs they had learned in Irene's childhood:

> *Summertime, and the living is easy.*
> *Fish are jumping and the cotton is high.*

Irene joined her mother in the song, their beautiful voices blending in harmony, carrying out over the blooming flowers in the backyard. Time seemed suspended on that crystal quiet morning.

In the stillness after the song, the Lord reminded Irene of a story He had once told her about a song played in the wrong key.

Irene could try to play this song and it sounded all right, but periodically she would hit a chord that sounded so disjointed it would ruin the whole melody.

But the Lord would change the key and fix the accidentals by His Word and His power, assembling the song so everyone could listen and appreciate its beauty. And people would say, "That's a beautiful song. How did you write it?"

And then she could say, "My life is a song that God wants to sing with me. It was disjointed and out of order, and no one wanted to listen to it. But now, because of Jesus, it's beautiful music. The notes fit together in a beautiful ballad with God's stamp of approval, saying, 'This is good! Use it!' But it was only useful after He fixed the sharps and flats and added the accidentals, bringing it into tune. And now it is all in harmony with the Holy Spirit."

As she thought about the story, her mother said, "I've had such a hard time forgiving people. I have held grudges when I shouldn't have. I've kept things in my heart long past the time I should have let them go. I've had a hard time forgiving William, because when I had cancer and almost died, he wasn't there for me. And now I wanted to make sure I had some time for you because I don't know what this sickness is going to do to you, honey. I don't know if you're going to be here in two years or what."

Irene reassured her that she would be okay: "Mom, God's taking care of me."

Her mother continued, "I wanted to talk to you before time passed and maybe I wouldn't have another chance. Honey, I'm so sorry about the hard times you had when you were a kid, when I wasn't there for you. And when you had to be the mom because I wasn't. I thank you for all the times that you were there and nobody else would lift a finger to help me.

"And I forgive you for taking grandma to Montana. I want you to understand that I couldn't help her because it hurt too bad to see my mom day after day, week after week slipping away. I needed her, but she couldn't help me any more. And I didn't know how to take care of her. I am glad you took care of her and helped her. I'm sorry I held a grudge against you for that."

And Irene said, "Momma, I'm so glad you understand."

Evelyn held up her hand to continue, "I need to tell you these things, Irene. Remember when you didn't know where your real dad was, and it upset you so much not to know him? I knew where he was all the time, but I thought he was such a bad man that he'd hurt you, and that's why I didn't tell you about him. Now that you're older, it's okay to know your dad. He's still not a really good person, but it's okay to know him.

"After we left him in Alaska, it broke my heart that we didn't have enough food or clothes or anything. But I didn't know how to fix it. I remember in Parkdale and Hood River when we didn't have enough food and I would allocate it, trying to space it out so there would be some food for each day. Then you kids would get into the peanut butter and I'd get angry with you because you were always hungry. You didn't understand that I was trying to have food for the next day, and I didn't know what to do."

"Then in anger and frustration, I'd spank you too hard. I know that. I wasn't kind to you. I didn't have any kindness in my life, so how could I know how to be kind to my kids?"

Irene's heart softened with understanding of the strain of her mother's situation.

"But Mom, there were good times too. Remember how God brought food to the door and we made that pipe cleaner angel? Remember how happy we were that day? And remember, you read the Bible to us?"

"That was just one day, Reenie," Evelyn said. "Let me finish what I need to say."

She went on, "I never got to know you as a person. When I was growing up, my parents would never come to any of my plays. They were always too busy or wouldn't take the time. Honey, I never came to hear you sing, did I?"

"No, Momma."

"I'm sorry."

"Momma, you know, I forgave you for all those things a long time ago. Jesus loves you, and I love you. You're going to make it, and we're going to be okay. We get to be friends now. No matter what, you've got to know that I forgive you and I love you and I accept you as my mom."

"I tried so hard, Reenie, but the days were fleeting. I couldn't hang on to them."

The words poured out like a dam breaking, "I know that the fire wasn't your fault. I have always thought it was really my fault for not being there with you. I never blamed you for the fire. I blamed Nina. She was the problem — not you, and not William. The hardest thing I've had to do in my life was to forgive that woman."

"Me too, Mom. But let's forgive her, okay? Not because it's good for her; it probably doesn't matter to her. But it's good for us."

Irene led them in prayer together, "Lord Jesus, I forgive Nina. And I love my mom. You are such a good God. Thank you for hearing us when we pray."

Then Evelyn asked, "Can you find it in your heart to forgive me, too? Could we find a way to go on from here?"

Irene said, "Momma, it's been years since I forgave you. I've told you before, but until today you have not been able to listen. But I'll tell you again, Momma, I love you, and I accept you, and I forgive you. Because Jesus has forgiven me, I have within me the ability to forgive you. Before that, I did not have the ability, because I, too, could not let go of grudges and hurts. I didn't know how to forgive or accept, but in the last year I've learned more tolerance and gained more understanding about who God is and how He wants us to live."

"Having this disease," she continued, "has taught me a lot. Maybe it will never go away, Ma, but I'm going to try with all that is within me to have a good life, despite how I feel — because

God is with me, helping me each day."

"Give Him a try, Momma. Just try letting Him into your life."

Evelyn turned her face away, "I'm not good enough to know Jesus. He's there. He's with me. I know He is. But I'm not good enough to be able to accept Him as my Savior. I've been too bad. I've done too many evil things to ever have Jesus in my life. My sin is too great for Him to forgive."

"Mom, Jesus is willing and able to forgive you from sin — any sin. Jesus can surely forgive you. But you also need to forgive yourself for all those things. And whether you understand it or not, you know that I have forgiven you."

"But beyond forgiving," Irene continued, "I also understand. You never had the resources that I had. You didn't have a husband that loved you and was by your side every day, like I do. William had to be gone all the time. You had all those kids by yourself.

"I have been very blessed, because I had Chris's support through all of this. And you need to know, Mom, that no matter what, I'll always love you and be here for you. If you need anything, any time you can depend on me."

Evelyn hugged Irene and together they wept tears of healing and rejoicing.

"Those are the most healing words I've ever heard in my life, Reenie. Thank you so much."

As the summer sun burned its way into August, Irene's health began to deteriorate. But this time her attitude was different. Now, in the understanding the Lord had given her of His purpose for her illness, she was better able to endure the agonizing pain in every any movement. As her vision blurred and her heart resumed its irregular pulse, she could look back on the remarkable changes of the past months and gain hope.

In the past, she could lead Bible study and worship, take care of the children, run the house, act as counselor to members of the church, and do anything else that arose. If someone needed her, she was obligated to fulfill their need. Now she could see that the Lord had never placed those demands on her.

Looking back, she could remember time after time when the Lord had encouraged her to slow down, to allow Him to work instead of trying to do everything herself. And now He had again taken her to the limits of her strength.

As she learned the difficult lesson of depending on Him, she could see that her striving to "fix" everything had often stood in His way. And in the healing she observed in the relationships within her family, she was learning to be satisfied with the perfection of His plans, to rest in Him, and to be truly be dependent on the Lord.

The Lord showed her that He gives opportunities to work for Him when He leads, but that He also wanted her to have a life. He showed her that everything in life is spiritual, not just church, or singing, or praying, or reading the Bible.

Now she realized that Jesus was in every part of her life — talking with her girls, planting flowers, watching a sunset. Jesus is what makes life so special. And without Him there is nothing.

When she returned to the doctor he prescribed another three weeks of antibiotics, a week longer than the first treatment. And she wondered if she would have to repeat treatment every few months for the rest of her life. The nurses had trouble finding veins to put the needles in. The pain was excruciating.

She asked God why He was allowing this suffering to continue: "I thought this was over God. You said in spring I would be better. Why do I have to do this again? I'm afraid, God."

And this time He gave her a clear answer.

"I have allowed this so that your family would come closer to Me. If they did not see that you could be vulnerable, that you were not always strong and happy, they would not listen to you."

"I want you to depend on Me and know that I am the One, I'll be your strength. I am the One who will fight for you. No matter what happens in your life I want you to stay close to Me."

And she asked Him, "Is that why I have Lyme disease?"

"That's one of the reasons," He answered. "But I want your family to know who you are. And if they only look at you when you are strong, they will not listen to you. I have opened a door, not just for your family, but for other people also."

"Okay, God. But I went through the disease," she argued. "Haven't I gone through enough? When does this all end?"

"Trust Me, Irene. Do you remember when you walked down those steep stairs in Hood River how frightened you were? You couldn't see one step in front of the other on your way down to the road. I want to take you on that journey again. If you trust Me and believe in Me, you will get to the end safely. I have a purpose in all of this."

And then He sang a song to her:

I'll be your kinsman redeemer
Your kinsman redeemer.
I'll do your fighting for you
Until the victory's won.
That you might know I am Father
The God of all creation
Your kinsman redeemer
Until the work is done.

As He sang, she realized that all her life He had chosen the songs that she sang for other people in church or in prison to sing back to her in her own times of need. How gracious He was to care for her with the very music that touched her heart.

For days He woke her up in the morning with that song. And even as waves of pain overwhelmed her body and her eyesight dimmed, she felt closer to God than ever before.

"If people would just realize how close He is," she thought, "they wouldn't feel lost and alone and afraid."

And then, as the antibiotics finally took hold, and once again pushed back the infection, returning her to a glowing feeling of health and well being, the Lord once again spoke to her heart.

He showed her a tunnel in the rock. Within the rock, deep cuts were made to free the rough diamonds from the bondage of a thousand tons of worthless stone. The raw gems were carefully retrieved from their weighty prison, but removing the jewel from the tunnel was only the first step. His desire is that His people — His diamonds — be completed, made into treasures of enormous worth.

"I created you to be a diamond, Irene," He said. "And in the diamond are many cuts. Each facet of the diamond is an aspect of your life. And the diamond that I have called you to be has many facets so that when My light shines on those facets it is highly reflected, so that people can see and know the beauty of the light, the shining light of Jesus. When one of My jewels catches the light, people look at it and are drawn to it. They are not drawn to the diamond itself, but to the light. But if My jewels are not cut correctly, the way I want them to be, they will not reflect My light."

And so He cuts the diamonds in different ways, unique angles for each of His unique children.

"And this is why I have cut you," He continued. "The cleaving process is painful, because My jewels are living beings. And some of the diamonds take a long time to cut correctly, because of their singular characteristics. But I plan every split to perfection so that My treasures will be priceless."

As she pondered the deep truth that the Lord was showing her, she prayed:

> *Thank you Lord for allowing me to have Lyme disease. Thank you for every day, every hour of pain that was necessary to bring me to this place. Thank you for your infinite wisdom in using even the worst incidents of my childhood to give me an understanding heart for the hurting world around me. My heart is so full I can barely express my praise for your Almighty goodness.*

EPILOGUE

Now then, I pray you, swear to me by the Lord, since I have shown you kindness, that you also will show kindness to my father's house, and give me a sure sign, And save alive my father and mother, my brothers and sisters, and all they have, and deliver us from death. And the men said to her, Our life for yours! If you do not tell this business of ours, then when the Lord gives us the land we will deal kindly and faithfully with you.

Joshua 2:12-14 AMP

You will show me the path of life; in Your presence is fullness of joy, at Your right hand there are pleasures for evermore.

Psalm 16:11 AMP

Now I know that the Lord saves His anointed; He will answer him from His holy Heaven with the saving strength of His right hand.

Psalm 20:6 AMP

He reached from on high, He took me, He drew me out of many waters. He delivered me from my strong enemy, and from those who hated and abhorred me; for they were too strong for me. They confronted and came upon me in the day of my calamity;

but the Lord was my stay and support. He brought me forth also into a large place; He was delivering me, because He was pleased with me and delighted in me. The Lord rewarded me according to my righteousness [my conscious integrity and sincerity with Him]; according to the cleanness of my hands has He recompensed me.

Psalm 18:16-20 AMP

Through It All

Through it all, through it all
I've learned to trust in Jesus
I've learned to trust in God
Through it all, through it all
I've learned to depend upon His Word.

I've had many tears and sorrows
I've had questions for tomorrow
There have been times I didn't know right from wrong
But in every situation
God gave blessed consolation
That my trials come to only make me strong.

I've been to lots of places
And I've seen a lot of faces
There have been times I felt so all alone
But in my lonely hours
Yes, those precious lonely hours
Jesus let me know that I was His own.

I thank God for the mountains
And I thank Him for the valleys
I thank Him for the storms He brought me through
For if I'd never had a problem
I wouldn't know that He could solve them
I'd never know what faith in God could do.

Sung by Andraé Crouch
© 1971 by Manna Music, Inc.
Used with permission.

I sit here on the porch of my home in Caldwell, Idaho and think about the strange and unique life that Jesus has led me through. And I am struck by the wonder of His nature, His character — a God willing to wait and watch His willful children go their own way, patiently anticipating the day they turn to Him for guidance, for His will. How often as a child I thought He had forgotten me.

There, by the rose bush, stands my tall, beautiful daughter Christy. She laughs merrily to herself, remembering some teen-age secret. She just graduated from high school and will enter college in the fall. She has the voice of an angel. And none of the evils of my youth has ever touched her. Looking at her, I see the hand of God.

Kneeling by the rabbit cage is fairest Emily, my strange and wonderful scientist — discoverer of bizarre bugs, examiner of tropical fish disease — consumed with wonder over the tiniest of nature's amazing treasures. She tosses her wild and magnificent hair out of her eyes, impatient with some new investigation. Looking at her, I see the hand of God.

Amanda stands with a friend from school, talking a mile a minute, repeating word for word a story she wrote for a school project, a narrative long ago turned in and graded, but undergoing yet another rewrite. Her mind moves so quickly, and when she learns to type, long novels of deep and intricate originality will pour out. They will be stories of elaborate imagination, but with great depth, understanding and sympathy for people. She is lovely and talented inside and out. And, once again, I see the hand of God.

And my precious Melissa sits by my side, playing with the dog and asking if I need any help with anything. She deftly weaves drying roses into a wreath to hang in the living room. She has such a sense of color, of texture, and she has only to imagine some artistic piece, and she can create it. Her exquisite smile is an endless joy to me. Once again, I see the hand of God.

And finally there is my Chris, my love, my dearest and closest earthly friend. A man of fiery temper, of tender heart, of fierce protection, and of soft understanding. A man of deep faith in Almighty God. A man of leadership, a believer in obedience. A man with a great love for Jesus. And a man of great patience with my daily struggle for wholeness.

In our four years here in Caldwell, we have yet to see God's promise fulfilled. I am reminded of the prophecy, "It will be a long time before you see the fruit, but you will see it with your eyes."

And I wonder why Chris never seems discouraged.

When I ask him about his incredible patience, he replies, "I look at missionaries that God has sent to foreign places who go and sometimes beat the streets for 20 years to get one convert. In America, we think if we don't grow a church to 250 in three years something is wrong. I think it has to do with obedience and submission. I think it has to do with hearing the voice of God, sticking it out and letting God give the increase."

I am humbled by his unshakable faith. Here he rests, in the hollow of the hand of God.

The message, the reason for writing this book, the story of my life, is simple. There is a great misconception about the nature of God, of how His plans are conceived and operated. Many of us believe that our faith will remove us from trials, difficulties in this earthly life.

Not only is this non-scriptural, it is untrue in every possible sense. God's message is the story of redemption, of deliverance.

In the Garden of Eden, God's original purpose was broken in pieces by our human desire to follow our own way. And since that time He has promised not to eliminate our obstacles, but to take our hand and walk with us, step by step, through them, weaving our way along secret paths known only by Jesus, paths that lead us safely through a perilous journey.

As the sun deepens the shadows on my back porch, Evelyn, my dear mother, steps outside carrying a tray of ice tea. My children rush to her, all talking at once, gently competing for her attention. As she turns to answer some unheard question, her answer carries over their chattering voices.

"The only thing that matters about that is Jesus," she says in her characteristic decisive voice. "Remember that He loves you, no matter what! Never forget that. By the time I learned to live, my whole life was almost over."

Tears of joy gather in my eyes, and the Holy Spirit warms my heart to hear those words. Never could I have imagined that my mother would know and love Him as I do. She is so beautiful and precious to me.

As a child, I chose to follow the leading of Christ, and as far as my understanding and knowledge goes, I followed that path (with some notable exceptions). But the people around me made other choices. And I lived my life in their midst, within the power of their choices.

And I think how God, in His Wisdom did not choose to remove me from starvation, child abuse, sexual abuse, dyslexia, or the other adversities of my youth. How mysterious are His ways.

I still live with the continual pain of arthritic inflammation, vestiges of the rickets and malnutrition of my childhood. I retain the residual effects of Lyme disease and additional repercussions of a compromised immune system, the continuing decline of cartilage in my spine and knees, causing further arthritis in my body. My thyroid is a disaster, and many days my body seems my worst enemy.

I don't think I ever really knew what life was about until I almost died in Weiser. God has changed me. I'm different than I was before. I am whole and filled with the joy that only knowing Him can give.

There is no day free of pain. But there is no day separated from Jesus. He has walked with me through every step, in every moment, in each situation of my life. He has never been more than a breath away, always willing to help and deliver. Many are the situations that have been diminished when I called for His help. He is, as always, a perfect gentleman, waiting for me to invite His loving intervention.

And as I have borne, with His grace, these impossible situations, person after person has seen Him through my eyes and come to know and love Him. As I have allowed Him to move, to use my life as a testimony to His never failing support, numerous people have come to know Him as Lord and Savior.

There has never been a situation, no possible event that He has not been willing, able, and ready to redeem, to restore, to repair in a way stronger than the original structure.

Today I love my mother more than I could have imagined. We have a deep relationship, based on forgiveness — an association that has been burned in the fires of hell, then restored with the tenderness and mercy available only in the personal hands of Almighty God.

I have a growing relationship with my biological father, lost almost since those early days in Alaska. God has given us a deep and caring love for each other, and we have shared the weeping of many tears over those sad and difficult days.

I speak often with my stepfather William, the man with the jovial deep laugh that was smothered out for a time, and we share a deep affection and love for one another.

Most of my sisters and brothers have come to know the saving grace of Jesus. He continues to heal them and give the peace and new life that only He can give.

As we began the writing of this book, my brother Michael told me, "Write the story, Reenie. Our story will help families to heal, and maybe their children won't get AIDS like I did."

And through Jesus, I was able to forgive and make peace even with the man who nearly single-handedly destroyed my family — the man who ravaged the innocence of my sisters and brothers. Before his death, I was able to forgive Grandfather Jess. In that action, my soul was free of him and that gnawing fear forever.

Perhaps the most difficult of all, I am able to forgive myself, for the times that I joined forces toward my own destruction, not fighting, allowing that victim mentality to overtake my very soul — and for other times when I took the reigns in my own hands and listened to my own voice, knowing that I was committing offenses capable of calling down the very wrath of Almighty God.

I remember those events as though I watched a movie. I can think of them without emotional annihilation, almost as if they happened to someone else instead of me. That is an enormous healing, the removal of pain from the numerous memories that scarred my youth.

> *Therefore, behold, I will allure her {Israel} and bring her into the wilderness, and I will speak tenderly and to her heart. There I will give her vineyards, and make the Valley of Achor or Troubling to be for her a door of hope and expectation. And she shall sing there and respond as in the days of her youth, and as at the time when she came up out of the land of Egypt.*
>
> Hosea 2:14,15 AMP

Being confident of this, that He who began a good work in you will carry it on to completion until the day of Christ Jesus.

Philippians 1:6 NIV

In this, my greatest hope, the most important knowledge, is that He isn't finished with me yet. This is His greatest promise, that He will take us on into His own perfection. We are perfectly faceted diamonds, protected always *In the Hollow of His Hand.*

Michael

Michael, I wish we could have been friends
You with your face against the wind
Not knowing how to bend . . .

Michael, I wish we could have been friends
Why won't you let me in?

When we were small
Off chicken coops we'd fly
Into grass waist high
Riding tree horses
We weren't so tall

Michael, I wish we could have been friends
You with your face against the wind

Climbing evergreens
We would escape on our childhood dreams
We could see a country mile
Oh, how I miss your smile

Sailing ship in an ocean of grass
Alice Through the Looking Glass
Days and years go by
I sit and wonder why . . .

Michael, we could have been friends!

Sweet memory of thee
Walking down the aisle with me
My dress in white
My face so bright

But now!
It's time to say good night

Michael, I wish we could have been friends
You with your face against the wind

But I can see
On heaven's shore
You dressed in white
Your face so bright

Michael, you calling,
"Reenie, Reenie, come home.
Forever friends we'll be.
Jesus has set me free."

Irene Taylor
March 1994

My prayer is that this story will help you realize how much Jesus loves you and how much He yearns to influence, touch and heal your life.

If you have never acknowledged Jesus Christ as your Savior, I invite you to pray this prayer. I promise that if you do this sincerely, it will change your life!

> *Lord Jesus, I admit that I have sin in my life and that I need your help. I believe that You died on the cross to deliver me from my sin. Please come into my life and accept me as Your child. Please be the Lord of my life. Please help me and let me know You person to person. I ask this in Jesus' name. Amen.*

If you sincerely prayed that prayer, you are now a member of the family of God — and a thousand angels in heaven are shouting, "Hosanna!"

The next steps are easy. Get a Bible, preferably one you can read, like the New International Version (NIV), or the Amplified Version (AMP), or "The Book."

Read it daily. It is God's love letter to us, His children.

And finally, find a good church that teaches the entire Word of God, and uses it as the absolute and only authority for faith and practice.

May God richly bless your life!

Irene Taylor

Irene Taylor
(author)

Seated: Melissa and Amanda
Standing: Emily, Chris, Irene, and Christy

STUDY
GUIDE
for
In the
Hollow of
His Hand

Study Guide Overview

This Bible Study is designed
to bring further insight
to the heart of a victim,
to help in the walk
from darkness
into light.

FEARS OF A CHILD

Fear of:

1. The dark:	Psalms 139:12
2. Life:	Deuteronomy 11:26-28
3. Family:	Psalms 45:8-11, John 21:17
4. Mother:	Psalms 27:10-4
5. Fear of fear:	Psalms 34:6-12
6. Trusting anyone, even God:	Psalms 56:11
7. Death:	Psalms 33:18-22
8. Never having enough:	Romans 15:13
9. Pain:	Psalms 28:7-9
10. Lack of control:	Galatians 5:18-22
11. Honesty:	Psalms 31:18
12. Abandonment, even by God:	Psalms 55
13. Not being heard:	Psalms 142:5-6
14. Not being believed:	Psalms 141:1-3

RIDGE

1. Some adults seem like children in adult bodies, unable to grow up. Why?

2. Is it easier to escape in sin than face life? Mark 7:14-16

3. How does a child grow up with the loss of a father's love?
Isaiah 1:2-9,
Malachi 2:10,
Luke 15:11-18

4. Who could Evelyn trust? Psalms 31:19

5. Who were the children's *real* parents? Psalms 33:18-19

ASTORIA

1. What do you think motivates people to do the things they
   do?   Isaiah 55

2. Without God's intervention, where would all of us be?

3. What does it take to build a house?   Ecclesiastes 3:11

4. How would you build your house?   Psalms 34:11

5. Are you born an alcoholic, or do you choose to be one?
                                               Proverbs 23:20-21

6. Do you have to know that you are lost to be found?
                                                      Luke 15:24

3

PALMER

1. Irene was originally named "Ione", but a nurse misspelled the name and she became Irene. Are names from the Lord? Go to the library and research the meaning of names of people in your family.   Isaiah 40:26

2. Why did Evelyn put Irene in the dresser?   Genesis 1:1-5, Psalms 19:12-13

3. Who is your good Samaritan?   Psalms 35:17-19

4. How were Shirley and Irene abandoned?   Psalms 36:7-9

5. Where did fear find its root?   Psalms 88:15, 32:4

6. Why didn't these parents have a bond with their children?   Psalms 121

VERNONIA

1. Why can clean sheets bring comfort to the heart of a child?   Revelations 19:6-9

2. Why was grandpa Ernie's kindness a door for the devil to harm the children?   Matthew 10:16

3. Why was there no protection for these children when even sheep protect their lambs?   Psalms 23, 119:117

4. Do some people believe that controlling the weak gives them god-like power?   Psalms 119:169-176

5. Evelyn wanted her dad to make her a special chair and have tea parties with her. How could she understand the lack in her life?   Proverbs 17:14

6. Why did Evelyn beat the children?   Psalms 34:9-11

7. Why do some children try to hard to please or perform for attention? Genesis 25:25-34

8. Where did Irene's mind set about music being her "god" begin? Ecclesiastes 7:5

9. Could Shirley and Irene ever be friends? Proverbs 18:19, Proverbs 17:17

10. Why do children look for love and kindness at any cost? Proverbs 4:2-4

HOOD RIVER

1. Did the fear of being alone drive Irene to Jesus?
   Isaiah 43:1-6

2. Who was Irene and Mike's mother?   Exodus 2:1-10

3. Why did Irene think she had to sing so loud for Jesus to
   hear?   Jeremiah 31:30-35

4. Why didn't Evelyn continue to seek God even after He
   helped her?   Proverbs 9:9-12,
                                    Deuteronomy 7:12-13

5. Where was God's mercy in this house?   Psalms 33:18-22

PARKDALE

1. Where do children learn common sense?

   Proverbs 5:23, 20:15

2. Why did Irene still trust her mother even after all of the beatings and abandonment? Psalms 69:20

3. How was Grandma Winfred a victim? Isaiah 42:22

4. How was Grandpa Jess setting-up each child?

   Proverbs 21:13, 16:27,
   Proverbs 22:22-25

5. Why do children need to know that they are worth loving? John 4:11-18

6. If Grandma loved the children, why didn't she help them?

   Psalms 39:9-13

7. If people tell a child that he or she is stupid, does the child live up to that expectation? Psalms 19:7-9

8. How do you view Irene at this point?

9. Why do all of us need hiding places?　　Psalms 90:1-4

10. Can we make our children targets for abuse?　Psalms 43

11. Why does the world seem to feed on people's weakness?
Psalms 40:14-17

12. Who was lost in Parkdale?　　　　Proverbs 18:21, 19-17,
Proverbs 19:19,
Proverbs 14:9, 26,31

Note: A concentration camp mentality implies survival at all
costs. If you don't obey all of the rules, you will die.
Proverbs 30:7-15,
Proverbs 15:11

13. Why is the desire for love such a strong "hook" for child abuse? Note: The victim mind set, "I deserve all this pain because I am a bad girl and a stupid fool."

Proverbs 15:16,17,
Proverbs 20:24, 16-22

14. Why do memories of physical or verbal abuse haunt people? Deuteronomy 8:2-3,
Lamentations 2:11-12

Can people be healed of those memories?

Proverbs 17:7-8,
Psalms 146:1-6,
Jeremiah 31:31-34

15. Why do children of abuse dislike themselves?

Proverbs 14:20,
Proverbs 19:7, 18:19

16. How would you feel if this happened to you or your children? Make a list of some of your feelings.   Isaiah 9:1-4,
Isaiah 49:15-16, 50:9

ASTORIA

1. Why did Mike always have his face against the wind?

    Lamentations 1:19,
    Psalms 103:15-16

2. Is there an end to evil?   Jeremiah 17:9-10

3. How can the circle of abuse stop?   Isaiah 51:1-4,
    Jeremiah 31:31-34

4. Were Shirley, Mike, or Irene ever truly children?

    Proverbs 17:6

5. Why do children of abuse become abusers?

    Proverbs 18:19

6. Why do abusive families sometimes "protect" their chil-
    dren?   Isaiah 59:1-4

7. How many times did Jesus save Irene's life in Astoria? Why?   Psalms 30:2-3,
                                                              Lamentations 3:21-23

8. Why didn't the school officials talk to Mike's mom and dad about him? Why did they think it was Irene's responsibility?   Lamentations 2:15-16

9. Why was music Irene's god?   Exodus 20:1-3

10. Why do children lie to get attention?   Proverbs 3:3-4

11. Did the children know right from wrong?   Proverbs 20:11

12. Could worse things happen to the children?
                                                              Psalms 140:1-7

BLUE RIDGE

1. Why didn't anyone believe Irene? Psalms 143:1-4

2. Why didn't Irene run away?

3. Could music ever hurt anyone? Lamentations 3:63-66,
Lamentations 4:1

4. How does the principle of free will apply to the death of Sam and David? Ecclesiastes 8:8-9

5. Why is the blame for things going wrong often shifted to the abused child? Psalms 25:17-22,
Proverbs 22:22-24

6. Will Irene ever trust anyone again? Psalms 20:7

7. How can Irene learn to forgive? Psalms 32:4-5,
Psalms 23

FRANKLIN STREET

1. Why didn't anyone comfort Irene after the fire?

   Psalms 18:16-18

2. Did Jesus reveal Himself as Irene's true father in the picture of Heaven? Revelations 22:1-6, John 20:17

3. If Sam and David hadn't died in the fire, what was their future? Isaiah 43:1-4

4. Why does lying come so easily to an abused child?

   Proverbs 15:3

5. Why did Irene take control of her life? Matthew 7:13-14

6. Did God send Chris to Irene? Proverbs 21:1-2

7. Why did God send Bob and Myrna to help Irene?

Proverbs 20:21

8. Why did Irene think abortion was the only answer?

Proverbs 17:11

9. What is God's heart about abortion?   Psalms 139

10. Why did Irene feel so guilty about wearing Grandma
    Ada's wedding dress?   Malachi 3:1-4

11. Why does God have to heal our past before we can truly
    live in the present?   Malachi 3:6-7

MARRIAGE

1. How can this marriage ever last?   Psalms 19:13-15

2. List three things God showed Irene to do as He healed
   Irene's mind and heart over the pain of her abortion?
                                                    Isaiah 41:10-13

3. How can obedience and forgiveness help in healing memories?   Ephesians 4:30-32

4. Make a list of all the people who have ever harmed you.
   Make a list of all the harm you have caused other people.
   Take both lists and forgive everyone, including yourself.
   In your heart, give back what you took from that person
   in mind, body, and spirit, then receive back what was
   taken from you in mind, body, and spirit.

5. Does God forgive every sin?   Psalms 103:10-15

6. Do all of us have the choice to do good or evil?
                                          II Thessalonians 3:2-5

7. Who is your father? Was he joyful when you were born?
                                          Psalms 139:13-17

8. When did God call Chris and Irene to the ministry?
                                          Romans 10:14, 8:29-31

SEATTLE

1. What was God teaching Chris and Irene at the
   Philadelphia Church?   Matthew 20:25-28

2. Why did the Taylor's not have enough food?
                                           Isaiah 40:11-12

3. List the bad memories that God healed in Irene's mind.

4. Why is trust the hardest lesson for Irene to learn?
                                           Psalms 3:2, 10:1, 17-18,
                                           Psalms 15:1-2

5. Is God calling you to be an Ida Simmons for someone?
                                           Proverbs 19:17

6. What did God renew in Irene through Chris's love for
   their daughters?   Joel 2:25-27

7. How does God use the areas that He has healed in your
   life to help others?   Isaiah 61:1-4

LITTLE CHURCH

1. When is "school" over for all of us?   Psalms 18:28-36

2. If you are a servant of God, can anyone take that position
   away from you?   Psalms 134

3. Why do Christians hurt one another?   Psalms 41:9-13

4. How can we trust man?   Psalms 20:6, 28:3,
                                                 Ecclesiastes 7:19-20

5. Have you ever been homeless?   Psalms 84

HELENA

1. Why did Chris and Irene go to the prison?   Isaiah 42:5-7

2. Why did they want to help the men there?   Isaiah 49:9

3. Why was Evelyn so upset with Irene for taking Grandma Ada to Montana?   Isaiah 59:9-11

4. Why did Irene say that she was glad that Evelyn was her mother?   Ephesians 6:2-3,
                                                  Proverbs 20:20

BOZEMAN

1. Why was having a house of her own so important to
   Irene?   Psalms 84:1-4

2. If onions have many layers, how many layers are there in
   the healing of the mind?   Psalms 19:12-13

3. At age 34, why did the thought of fire still make Irene
   cry?   Isaiah 54:16-17

4. What were the little things Jesus talked about when He
   danced with Irene in heaven?   Psalms 30:9-12

5. Why was it so hard for the Taylors to leave Bozeman?

WEISER

1. Why did the Taylors go to Weiser?

2. What sin did Irene commit for God to give her Lyme's disease?   Psalms 116:5-10

3. Why did Irene's mother come to Weiser?   Proverbs 19:20

4. Is long-term illness a result of lack of faith or sin?
                                    Psalms 31:11-16

5. Why was Irene's dance in Heaven so important?
                                    Psalms 30:9-12

6. What did God teach Irene during her illness?
                                    Psalms 119:124-125,
                                    Psalms 18:28-30

7. What did God teach the people at the Weiser church?

Psalms 27:13-14

8. Why can God be trusted?

Psalms 90:15-17,
Psalms 118:8-9,
Psalms 33:16-22

9. Did the Taylors leave Weiser too soon?

CALDWELL

Isaiah 26:1-4, 54:11-13